Mira Fels

Making Sense of Corruption in India

Interethnische Beziehungen und Kulturwandel

Ethnologische Beiträge zu soziokultureller Dynamik

herausgegeben von

Prof. Dr. Jürgen Jensen, Universität Hamburg

Band 64

Mira Fels

Making Sense of Corruption in India

An Investigation into the Logic of Bribery

LIT

Cover photograph by: Shantala Fels

Bibliographic information published by the Deutsche Nationalbibliothek
The Deutsche Nationalbibliothek lists this publication in the Deutsche Nationalbibliografie; detailed bibliographic data are available in the Internet at http://dnb.d-nb.de.

ISBN 978-3-8258-1384-0

A catalogue record for this book is available from the British Library

© LIT VERLAG Dr. W. Hopf Berlin 2008
Auslieferung/Verlagskontakt:
Fresnostr. 2   48159 Münster
Tel. +49 (0)251–62 03 20   Fax +49 (0)251–23 19 72
e-Mail: lit@lit-verlag.de   http://www.lit-verlag.de

Distributed in the UK by: Global Book Marketing, 99B Wallis Rd, London, E9 5LN
Phone: +44 (0) 20 8533 5800 – Fax: +44 (0) 1600 775 663
http://www.centralbooks.co.uk/acatalog/search.html

Distributed in North America by:

Transaction Publishers
New Brunswick (U.S.A.) and London (U.K.)

Transaction Publishers
Rutgers University
35 Berrue Circle
Piscataway, NJ 08854

Phone: +1 (732) 445 - 2280
Fax: + 1 (732) 445 - 3138
for orders (U. S. only):
toll free (888) 999 - 6778
e-mail:
orders@transactionspub.com

For my husband Kai Fels.

'The most wonderful of all things in life is the discovery of another human being with whom one's relationship has a growing depth, beauty and joy as the years increase' (Hugh Walpole).

Acknowledgements

Thanks to my family for support, encouragement and love. My sister Shantala Fels, for understanding me, and for listening. My father Jaspal Singh Fels, for giving me power and drive. My mother Regina Fels, for giving me the key to inner peace. And my family-in-law, Elisabeth, Uschi, Rolf, Heike and Abraxas Renziehausen, for giving me a second home.

Thanks to my teachers, most of all to (Assistant) Professor Dr. Martin Sökefeld, my tutor, who has inspired my studies and helped me to search answers to my many queries.

Thanks to my Indian friends, family and informants during my research in 2004, which has led to the enquiry presented in this paper. Especially Pushpa Singh, Mukat Singh and Praveen Kaushal, whose dedication and uprightness impressed me.

Thanks to Laura Glauser, Cristian Alvarado-Leyton, Anna Katharina Sanner and Tracey Zinn-Williams for stimulating discussions and proof-reading.

Thanks to all my friends, and to my teacher and fellow students of the classical Indian dance Odissi that gave me respite, new strength and joy. Especially Gudrun Märtins, Vanessa Jeroma, Anastasia Fedjanina, and Bianca and Raja Percic.

Finally, thanks to Adalbert Schlag and the Friedrich-Ebert-Foundation, which has financed, encouraged and enriched my studies.

Preface

Corruption is a major problem in the present, global world. Earlier, it was mostly seen as a shortcoming of so-called "third world" countries. From a Western perspective, corruption is generally condemned and the elites of "developing" countries are frequently accused of thriving on the riches that they illegally snatch from their societies, the poorest section included. Yet moral absolutism is inappropriate. Recent developments, relating for instance to the German company *Siemens*, made utterly clear that the "first world" is involved in corruption, too, and that practices of corruption "here" and "there" are ultimately two sides of the same coin.

Corruption is a very complex phenomenon. It has economic, political and ethical aspects and is simultaneously a global and a local issue. In the last few years, corruption has become an important topic for social anthropology. As corruption has to do with the gap between formal rules and actual practices, it is a paradigmatic subject of political anthropology that asks how formal and informal practices and positions of power are interrelated and reflect upon one another.

The present work deals with corruption in India. Corruption is regarded as endemic in Indian society. According to *Transparency International*, the international NGO combating corruption, India ranks 88th among 144 countries and achieves a score of only 2.9 on a 0 to 10 scale, on which 10 indicates the "cleanest" score and 0 the most corrupt.[1] Yet although such rankings certainly have their value, to simply condemn India as a corrupt country and society would be beside the point.

The purpose of Mira Fels' study is "to make sense of corruption". Making sense of ideas, practices and aspects of culture and society, i.e. making them understandable, is the goal of the anthropological endeavour. From the perspective of anthropology, "making sense" of something does not mean to defend or excuse it. It means that there may be much more about a social phenomenon than what appears at first inspection, and that the task is to uncover hidden relations, conditions, meanings and also constraints.

In this vein Mira Fels approaches the ethnography of corruption in India. After situating the topic within global conditions and the context of the Indian political system, she starts by looking at corruption "from below", asking how it is experienced by those who are the victims of corruption, mostly

---

[1] Transparency International ranking of 2005, see
http://www.tiindia.in/data/files/CPI%202005.pdf (accessed 14 May 2008).

in their dealings with bureaucracy. Drawing on various studies as well as on her own fieldwork, she uncovers a succession of allegations: While "common people" hold bureaucrats responsible for corruption, bureaucrats pass the responsibility on to politicians. Focusing on the rural context she shows that the extension of the state into all social realms through programmes of development also extends opportunities for corruption.

The study shows how actors in Indian society are entangled in hierarchical relations of social, economic and political inequality that breed corruption, yet also how resistance against corruption takes place in local context. Further, Mira Fels argues that corruption does not originate from remnants of "traditional society" like caste and family relationships, but that "modern" forms of governance and market relations play a significant role. Significantly, she also shows that programmes of liberalisation and privatisation may not be the remedy against corruption as which they are frequently celebrated. Instead, they may contribute to the growth of corruption by further reducing transparency and public accountability. By exposing the complexity of corruption and also by questioning apparently simple remedies, this rich study certainly contributes to "making sense" of corruption in India.

Dr. Martin Sökefeld
Assistant Professor of Social Anthropology
University of Bern

I. Talking About Corruption: Introduction — 1

1. Outline & Literature Review — 2

2. Global Consensus on Corruption? — 3
2.1. The End of the Cold War — 4
2.2. The Rise of Democracy — 5
2.3. Economic Globalisation — 5
2.4. Washington Consensus on Corruption — 6
2.5. Engineering Corruption — 7
2.6. Different Strategies Against Corruption — 8

3. The Politics of Defining Corruption — 9

4. Approaches to the Study of Corruption — 12
4.1. Socio-Cultural Explanations — 12
4.2. Economic Considerations — 14
4.3. Legalistic & Political Approaches — 16
4.4. Why an Anthropology of Corruption — 18

II. Setting: The Indian State — 20

1. Ideas of India — 20
1.1. Social & Economic Development — 20
1.2. Politics - Democracy in Diversity — 20

2. Performance of Democracy — 21

3. Performance of Economic Development — 23
3.1. Industry & Protectionism — 24
3.2. Peasants & Land Redistribution — 25
3.3. Economic Populism & Liberalisation — 26
3.4. Access to Natural Resources — 28
3.5. Livelihoods in the Unregistered Sector — 29

4. Welfare State? – Selected Public Services	29
4.1. Educational Facilities	30
4.2. Health Care	32
4.3. Development Programmes	33
4.4. Conclusion: The State of Public Services	34

III. Making Sense of Corruption in India — 35

1. Marginalised Citizens & Resistance — 36

1.1. Citizens & Corruption	36
1.1.a. Public Services in Uttar Pradesh	36
1.1.b. A Villager's Access to Development	41
1.1.c. A Social Movement in Rajasthan	43
1.2. Citizens & Corruption: Findings	47
1.2.a. Public Services for Whom?	48
1.2.b. Who has to Bribe?	50
1.2.c. Political Reasons	50
1.2.d. Information & Empowerment	51
1.2.e. How Citizens Handle Public Services	54
1.2.f. Officials' and Politicians' Reactions	55
1.2.g. Attitudes Towards the State	56
1.2.h. Citizens Making Sense of Corruption	58

2. The Bureaucracy — 59

2.1. Introduction to the Indian Bureaucracy	59
2.2. Bureaucrats & Corruption	62
2.2.a. How two Land Agents Collect Bribes	62
2.2.b. Inspecting a Development Scheme	65
2.2.c. Corruption in Canal Irrigation	68
2.3. Bureaucrats & Corruption: Findings	75
2.3.a. Prices, Performance & Insecurity	76
2.3.b. Procedural Power & Hierarchy	78
2.3.c. Transfers	80

2.3.d. Good Governance vs. Scarcity	82
2.3.e. Costs of Corruption	86
2.3.f. Political Pressures & Consumerism	86
2.3.g. Morality & Reforms	89
2.3.h. Who Sets the Limit?	92
2.3.i. Bureaucrats Making Sense of Corruption	93

3. Political Players' Quest for Influence — 94

3.1. Introduction to Indian Politics	94
3.2. Politics & Corruption	96
3.2.a. Political Change in Andhra Pradesh	97
3.2.b. Five Indian Villages in 1999-2000	106
3.2.c. Personalised Power in Bihar	108
3.2.d. Participation in West Bengal	110
3.3. Politics & Corruption: Findings	111
3.3.a. Economic Power & Labour Dependency	112
3.3.b. Elite Competition & Accommodation	113
3.3.c. Polticial Rhetoric & the Media	116
3.3.d. Personalised Power	118
3.3.e. Brokers & Contractors	121
3.3.f. Party Politics & Participation	124
3.3.g. Villager's Political Mobilisation	126
3.3.h. Politicians Making Sense of Corruption	129

IV. Summary & Conclusion — 130

V. Literature — 136

I. Talking About Corruption: Introduction

Upon my first encounters in 2004 with three development organisations in India, where I sought to gather inspiration for this master's thesis, I was struck by the vast gap that seemed to exist between formal rule of law and democracy on one side and on the other side, the informal rules of how things actually seemed to work.

I had spent ten days with the 'Society for the Promotion of Himalayan Indigenous Activities' in Dehradun. The organisation worked with the Van Gujjar, a nomadic indigenous group living in the Shivalik forest in Northern India. The Van Gujjar earn their living by selling milk, but spend as much as fifty percent of their meagre income to bribe low-ranking forest officials (Feiring, Brigitte et al. 2002: 10). Most of the bribery is due to their lack of valid permits for the buffaloes they own, but also for other charges which seem to be made up, for instance, cutting Bharbar Grass in the forest, a violation the villagers allegedly also perform, without being fined.

In Amapurkashi, a village in Uttar Pradesh with 1700 inhabitants, I stayed with 'The Society for Agro-Industrial Education' for five weeks. The students from the local college openly told me that they had to bribe to get government jobs. Besides studying, they worked and saved money for this. When the sweeper applied for a second job, he was asked to pay a bribe several times his monthly salary. I was told that there was corruption at all levels, at the police stations, in the education system and in politics. A bright young student from a poor family, Mukesh, told his sister that in India, no matter how hard he tried, he could not get anywhere without money, power and connections to powerful individuals (Fels 2005).

In an article online, Utkarsh Kansal remarked:

> 'It is impossible for a common man to own a roof, provide good education to his children and hope for a peaceful retirement in India using normal and honest means. One has to bribe someone to get a good education, to get a deserving job and to avail [of] services [to] which one is entitled as being a citizen of India' (Kansal 2001: 1).

I asked myself what such a situation would do to the state's legitimacy in the eyes of its citizens and employees. What affect does it have for their trust in the way the state is organised, if politicians constantly promise development and democracy with equal chances for all while the opposite seems to be true?

I.1. Outline & Literature Review

When studying the literature about corruption, I found that most of it had a normative, etic approach to the subject which was hardly ever questioned, because of the moral tone of the discussion. In this paper I seek to look at the emic perspective from an ethnographic point of view instead. Much of the literature seemed to reduce the phenomenon to simple equations. With some notable exceptions (Krastev 2003, Haller & Shore 2005, Wade 1982, Gupta 1995 & 2005, Parry 2000, Joshi & Mander 1999) most authors seemed to grasp neither the complexity of, nor the power politics intermingled in the practice – and discussion – of corruption. My aim is to challenge these over-simplified explanations and contrast them with the observed complexities within India by looking at those involved with the phenomenon.

I want to 'make sense' of corruption in order to arrive at an understanding of the phenomenon. To do so, I will look at corruption as experienced in India. The most relevant players I identified are: marginalised citizens, bureaucrats and politicians. I contend that corruption is a subject whose exact meaning is contested. I want to interrogate the ways in which the participants named above relate to each other, and attempt to make sense of corrupt behaviour, and also look at how the discourse about corruption becomes 'a site for other conflicts in the economic and political realms' (Pavarala 1996: 15).[2]

In the introduction, I will first talk about the global relevance the subject corruption has been assigned. Subsequently, I will examine the one most paradigmatic definition of corruption in order to show how politics are involved in choosing one definition over another. In the same chapter, I will briefly discuss a few selected theoretical approaches to the study of corruption, in order to show what perspectives anthropological, or more generally, empirical studies can add to the existing body of literature, namely an insider's emic as opposed to a normative, etic perspective.

The second chapter will be an introduction to the Indian situation. Since the post-colonial promises of democracy, removal of poverty and economic development are the background against which the performance of the Indian state is measured, with corruption frequently being blamed for poor outcomes, I will first address the social and economic state of the majority of Indians today, with a special focus on the marginalised. I will look at how their situation, their relationship with the state and the perspectives upon it have changed since Independence in 1947.

---

[2] I will not focus in detail on other factors like institutional constraints, lawmaking or economic aspects, because they have been given a lot of attention in the literature (chapter I.4).

In the ethnographic part of my paper, I will first try to show how corruption is experienced and reflected upon by common people. As far as this can be achieved a special focus will be given on poorer or marginalised sections of the population – as it is described in the publication of the economists Peter Lanjouw and Nicholas Stern (1998) and in a paper by anthropologist Akhil Gupta (1995). Additionally, I will look at a paper written by Abha Joshi and the former civil servant Harsh Mander (1999) about a social movement in Rajasthan. Since 'common citizens' mostly encounter corruption in their interactions with the bureaucracy, I will follow their lead and look at the bureaucrats more closely in the following chapter using ethnography by Gupta (1995, 2005) and a study of corruption in canal irrigation in South India by Robert Wade (1982). In turn, bureaucrats often hold politicians responsible for high levels of corruption, I will explore politics in the fourth chapter. Here, I will draw upon an ethnography of political development in a South Indian village by Marguerite Robinson (1988) and on a book published by the geographers Stuart Corbridge, Glyn Williams, Manoj Srivastava and René Véron in 2005.

The last findings included in the studies relied on data gathered between 1981 and 2001[3], a time span of twenty years. The research was conducted in different regions of India, which are geographically remote from each other (for a short discussion of regional differences, refer to chapter III). All the same, they belong together politically, historically and bureaucratically. Not all of the studies focused on corruption, as it is rather a new subject in the social sciences, and in anthropology in particular, nor were all of them written by anthropologists. With one exception (compare chapter III.1.1.c), however, all authors gathered their data during ethnographic field researches. I chose their studies, because they examined social, bureaucratic and political processes either with a great comprehensiveness or with an ethnographic depth which other literature lacked and because they looked at the phenomenon from a variety of different angles. Comparing the qualitative data and putting it into context, I hope to generate some general hypothesis' about the phenomenon of corruption which could then be tested by a more structured and comprehensive work.

I.2. Global Consensus on Corruption?

'The last decade of the 20th century was remarkable for the global explosion of interest in corruption' (Krastev 2003: 107).

Corruption turned into one of the most widely discussed policy issues among all kinds of people: 'World leaders, journalists, and ordinary citizens

---

[3] For further elaboration, see chapter III.

[became] simply obsessed with corruption' (Krastev 2003: 105). Patrick Glynn et al. described the rise of the subject with dramatic metaphors:

> 'Corruption ha[d] been transformed from a predominantly national or regional preoccupation to an issue of global revolutionary force ... the worldwide backlash against corruption ... swept like a firestorm across the global political landscape ... no region and hardly any country, [was] immune' (1997: 1).

Almost no one would dare to question the following statement:

> 'Outside of war, corruption poses probably the greatest single threat to democracy' (Haller & Shore 2005: 10).

The 'world's oldest part-time professions: proffering and accepting bribes' (Glynn et al. 1997: 1), which had been around for centuries, were suddenly in the international spotlight. Whereas corruption had long attracted a great deal of attention, it had been a 'non-issue in the field of international politics' until rather recently (Krastev 2003: 110). The anti-corruption consensus seemed to unite all those that normally stood on opposite sides: left and right, liberal and conservative, globalisation and anti-globalisation (Krastev 2003: 106). The question is: why. There are several possible answers. Broadly speaking, there are five categories of explanation: the first one is historical, and holds the end of the cold war responsible, the second, interconnected political explanation talks about the rise of democracy and civil society, the third, economic argument focuses on globalisation, the fourth blames US interests and international credit institutions. The fifth one, finally, emphasises the changed approach to the study of corruption in the social sciences. I will analyse these explanations one by one to show how historical, political, economic and scientific developments have together led to the rise of a new topic in international relations. It will be emphasised that changing political, economic and legal circumstances also lead to a redefinition of elite interests, as elites need to employ new strategies to safeguard their political and economic power base. Following Krastev I suggest that the convergence of these redefined interests led to the emergence of corruption as a global issue.

I.2.1. The End of the Cold War

What Eric Wolf (1977: 175-176) had predicted, namely that the end of the Cold War would also alter the informal arrangements necessary during this period turned out to be true, according to many authors (Hauschild 2000, Glynn et al. 1997: 9-11, Krastev 2003: 108). After the end of the Cold War in 1989, Hauschild argued, Wolf's predictions proved right when in Belgium, Bolivia, China, Yugoslavia and South Africa common people, public interest organisations and politicians called for a new transparency and disempowered the old patron-rulers (Hauschild 2000). The end of the ideological clash also meant the end of political hypocrisy, as Krastev (2003: 108) put it. There was no longer any reason to support governments simply to keep them from joining 'the other side'. Rulers as well as development policies needed a new foundation to justify their behaviour, especially in the formerly Communist countries where massive privatisation took place, often accompanied by suspicions of corruption. The new public focus was thus on moral values and integrity (Krastev 2003: 108).

I.2.2. The Rise of Democracy

Another explanation concerns the rise of democracy. In 1996 the human rights organization 'Freedom House' classified sixty-one percent of the world's countries as democratic – nineteen percent more than ten years earlier (Glynn et al. 1997: 11). Democracies are not necessarily less corrupt than other regimes (Krastev 2003: 109), but 'electoral campaigns are exceptional situations where issues known to everybody and normally given little weight may suddenly become charged with importance' (Haller & Shore 2005: 13). Riding the wave of this trend, the media and civil society in many democratic societies have also become more independent and often exposed corrupt leaders and campaigned for anti-corruption measures (Krastev 2003: 9). Gupta points out that states' quest for legitimacy in the interstate system may be one of the reasons why allegations of corruption are taken more serious today:

> 'The discourse of corruption varies a great deal from one country to another, dependent as it is on particular historical trajectories and the specific grammars of public culture. Taking the international context of nation-states into account, however, brings their substantial similarities into sharp relief. In order that a state may legitimately represent a nation in the international system of nation-states, it has to confront at least minimally to the requirements of a modern nation-state. The tension between legitimacy in the interstate system and autonomy and sovereignty is intensifying for nation-states with the continued movement toward an increasingly transnational public sphere' (Gupta 1995: 393).

I.2.3. Economic Globalisation

The third explanation is all about the increasing interconnectedness of global markets (Krastev 2003: 109). The interdependence of markets means that corruption can have effects on the world economy. Passas showed in 1994 that when the corrupt Bank of Credit and Commerce Internationally went bankrupt in 1991, the social security funds of Gabon were entirely wiped out. The digitalisation of the international finance system means that millions of dollars can be moved with a mouse click, literally.

> 'The volume flowing through this network is almost incomprehensible – well over $ 1 trillion a day in foreign exchange transactions only' (Glynn et al. 1997: 14).

Additionally, there is extensive worldwide cooperation between companies which is becoming more difficult to control. 'The very concepts of national products, national firms and national markets are crumbling'. Interfirm Alliances, however, depend on mutual trust which can easily be jeopardised by cases of corruption. Thus, these new global realities may also inhibit corruption (Glynn et al. 1997: 12-15). The same international inter-connectedness makes it easier to 'name and shame' corrupt companies or governments, for instance on the internet that even totalitarian states like China find hard to control. Several journalists discovered 'blogs', online diaries, as forums in which to write. The internet police was never as fast as they were. By the time the censors finally succeeded in deleting the text, many people had read it already (Blume 2006). Also, the international digitalised financial trade could potentially be controlled much better, as was proven after the destruction of the World Trade Center in New York on the 11th of September 2001. The US government accessed data from the 'Society for Worldwide Interbank Financial Telecommunication' (Swift), which coordinated financial transactions for a total of 7,800 banks in 200 countries in order to find terrorists (Spiegel Online 27.6.2006). Access to this data could also be used to control the transactions of corrupt top politicians, if an international agreement could be reached.

I.2.4. Washington Consensus on Corruption

The fourth explanation differs from the more or less organic and rather optimistic arguments about the course our world is taking. The Eastern European political scientist Krastev argues that

> 'the new anti-corruption rhetoric … came as a response to changes in the politics of international trade; … it was the politics of international financial institutions that resulted in the new visibility of corruption and in the new conceptualization of its role' (Krastev 2003: 110).

He argues that three groups of powerful actors, the United States' State Department, multinational corporations and the World Bank, and the convergence of their differing interests were the reasons why corruption became a global issue.

In 1977, after the Watergate and Lockheed-scandals, the American Foreign Corruption Practices Act outlawed bribing of foreign officials by Americans. Businessmen complained that this law was undermining their chances in the 'bribe-expecting environments of the third world' (Krastev 2003: 112). Under the 'trade-minded' Clinton administration the US state department started pressuring its OECD partners and European governments to introduce similar legislation (Glynn et al. 1997: 17, Krastev 2003: 112).

After the Cold War, multinationals had reasons of their own to start condemning corruption. They had considered corruption to be useful in the 1960s and 70s, because it helped them to open up the economies of developing countries. But after the end of the Cold War, conditional loans from the International Monetary Fund forced most governments to open their markets regardless of this. Furthermore, multinationals found that in post-Communist countries they were outsiders - whereas in the developing world multinationals which had been linked to the colonisers had local knowledge of when and how to bribe whom. In countries such as Russia

> 'laws were (kept) vague on purpose and their explicit goal was to keep foreigners out.' (Krastev 2003: 113-114).

The third party that 'discovered' the subject of corruption were the Bretton Woods Institutions: the World Bank and the International Monetary Fund. During the Cold War, they tried to keep developing countries in the capitalist block by offering them cheap credit and avoided touching sensitive issues. After 1989, however, the institutions had to redefine their role and confront growing criticism of their failures in Russia. So Wolfensohn, former head of the World Bank, decided, as he told Rose-Ackermann in 1999,

> 'that I would redefine the 'C' word, not as a political issue, but as something social and economic' (Haller & Shore 2005: 19).

And soon the World Bank had established itself as the new authority on anti-corruption measures, which, as Steven Sampson argued, is actually equal to the neoliberal agenda (Haller & Shore 2005: 19) long pursued by these institutions, advocating a limited state and the belief that unrestrained markets work for the best of societies (see chapter III.2.3.d for a brief evaluation).

I.2.5. Engineering Corruption

The last party that has been vital in making the issue of corruption 'fit for the global stage' is social sciences. Corruption had long been regarded as a moral problem and thus largely been ignored by social researchers. Some followed Robert Merton's lead, who argued that corruption can be beneficial for development and cannot be analysed outside its concrete context. The 'major turn' occurred, when corruption came to be seen as rational, economic behaviour that depended upon incentives. Thus,

> 'putting incentives right was declared sufficient to reduce endemic corruption' (Krastev 2003: 120).

The discourse on corruption was decontextualised and became normative. Anthropologists, who had long argued that Western norms were not unproblematically applicable to other societies, found themselves attacked by exactly the 'natives' they had sought to protect, because their argument had meanwhile been turned around and was used as a

> 'pretext for treating these societies as inferior with respect to development and economic growth' (Krastev 2003: 120).

The final PR-coup was launched by the public interest organisation Transparency International in 1994. Using estimates similar to those a company named Political Risk Services had regularly prepared for businessmen, they published the first 'Corruption Perception Index', which ranked countries according to how corrupt executives from multinational companies perceived them to be. The vague data base and methodical critique notwithstanding, the index has come to be used like 'hard data'. Thus economists had, 'on the basis of the legitimacy enjoyed by any quantative type of analysis' launched an enormously successful PR-tool, while at the same time 'radically marginali[sing] non-economic discourses on corruption'.

This global approach de-politicised the issue, and turned it into a problem for experts, whose preferred anti-corruption measures can be contrary to the ideas of local groups, as will be discussed below (Krastev 2003: 121-125).

I.2.6. Different Strategies Against Corruption

We can conclude that several reasons are to be held responsible for the rise of corruption to a topic that is now internationally discussed and has become charged with political importance: the end of the Cold War, the rising number of democratically governed states, where elections are held on a regular base, a transnational public sphere, increased economic interdependence, a convergence of the redefined interests of US businessmen, multinationals and the World Bank and last, but certainly not least, the new definition of corruption as rational behaviour based on incentives and the successful PR-launch of an index that measures the perception of corruption by Transparency International.

The fact that so many players agree something must be done about corruption and that almost no one seems to question the 'moral crusade', should not lead us to believe they are all talking about exactly the same thing. As demonstrated above, different interests are involved in defining a phenomenon as a problem which can and should be tackled. These may lead to different strategies to fight corruption, because there might be a dissension about what problems corruption entails.

Krastev (2003: 123-124) broadly categorised two different 'corruption-arguments': the democracy argument and the free market argument. The democracy argument has mostly been propagated by subaltern groups and civil society insisting that the power of big money and the market has to be controlled by the state, which, in turn, should become more democratic. The free market argument, in contrast, is emphasised by companies, governments and international institutions. It emphasises that it is big governments who foster corruption. In their view, therefore, the state needs to be reduced. While 'it is easy to reconcile the two arguments rhetorically', you can hardly at the same time reduce and enlarge the power of the state. Krastev argues that civil society has not yet awoken to the reality that their own arguments have been turned around to further economic interests. On the other hand, Drèze and Sen (2006: 21) caution us, that the size of the state apparatus is not necessarily an indicator of the quality of its performance and that it is quality, and not size, which matters when assessing the role of the state.

In this paper, I look at the different interests and pressures involved in the practice and discussion of corruption within India. Before proceeding to the Indian case, I will discuss one widely used definition of corruption, followed by introducing selected theoretical approaches to the study of corruption, which have informed my perspective as well as other author's way of viewing the phenomenon.

I.3. The Politics of Defining Corruption

As stated above, my inquiry starts from the assumption that corruption, as well as development, and democracy, are terms whose meanings are contested. Therefore, I will not try to find a definition valid only for my paper.[4] Instead, the different interpretations of the phenomenon are precisely what I am interested in. Still, it seems to be important to discuss at least briefly one of the definitions[5] widely used in the academic world in order to

---

[4] Even if I wanted, I couldn't do so, most of the case studies I use do not specifiy their or their informant's definition of corruption.
[5] Other definitions have either experimented with the term 'public opinion' or 'public interest', which is also briefly discussed below, or been built around the

emphasize my point, namely, that there is a need to look at which interests lead players to choose a certain definition.

The World Bank, one of the biggest players in the world of development and policy reforms, which has launched a global 'crusade' against corruption in 1998 (Shore & Haller 2005: 18), defined corruption as 'the abuse of public office for private gain' in 2002. As Shore and Haller point out, this definition reduces the phenomenon to stray individuals in public office settings (Shore & Haller 2005: 2). Privatising public sector undertakings, a measure promoted by the World Bank long before the talk about corruption began, thus became a prime solution, because, by definition, corruption only existed in public offices, not in private companies. The private sector was ignored (Shore & Haller 2005: 18).

While more recent definitions, which emerged after corruption scandals at the Wall Street and the US giant Enron, extended the definition to include any sort of 'entrusted authority', for example that of a board chairman (Sampson 2005: 106), other doubts remain. What if corruption was not only individual misbehaviour, as the definition assumed? It might also be considered an institutional or systemic phenomenon, an assumption Haller & Shore draw from looking at Jane and Peter Schneider's (2005) comparison between organised crime and corporate scandals: They

> 'raise the question whether organisational crime, extortion and illegal trafficking are not full-fledged elements of the workings of capitalism as such' (Haller & Shore 2005: 5).

Also, corruption as a systemic problem might not be hidden from the public eye, but in fact be well known about. As Gore Vidal wrote about the political system in the USA in 1999:

> '[People] know that public offices are bought by those who can pay and denied to all the rest, that politicians are better identified with their corporate ancestry than voting base' (Haller & Shore 2005: 12).

Schneider and Schneider (2005: 30) also pointed out that all over the world the powerful and wealthy were least likely to be punished for crimes such as corruption, because they had more resources to defend themselves and were more influential in formulating laws and rules in the first place. Italy's premier Berlusconi, to name just one example, had the law changed so that his previously 'illegal' practice of book-keeping was redefined as legal (Haller & Shore 2005: 2).

---

notion of a market-centred logic permeating into public offices (Krastev 2003: 118; Theobald 1990: 1-18).

Another problem is the question of whether a specific act is in fact for 'private gain' or, rather, in the interest of the 'public'. Who is to decide and thereby speak for the public interest at large? As Haller and Shore pointed out, this is precisely the question 'over which democratic politics are fought' (Haller and Shore 2005: 5).

Following Weber (1976: 126-128), incumbents of public office are expected to distinguish sharply between their private interests and the public role they assume. This makes corruption a measure of just how well a society distinguishes between these spheres (Rose-Ackermann, 1996: 365, Theobald 1990: 2). But the distinction is by no means as universal as the definition would have us believe. Gupta raises the question whether the idea of a

> 'role-fulfilling, disinterested professional occupying a location in an organizational structure solely due to professional competence and merit' is not 'as much a figment of modern imagination as his or her imagined contrast' (Gupta 2005: 8)

In fact, who can completely cease to be a regular human being with likes, dislikes, personal needs, interests and ambitions as soon as he enters his workplace? In India, but I suggest also in other settings, though certainly with varying degrees

> 'officials (like ... the Village Development Worker) are seen as thoroughly blurring the boundaries between 'state' and 'civil society' (Gupta 1995: 384).

So is there something wrong with the development worker or is it the definition that is the problem? Gupta doubts the correctness of the definition:

> 'It is perhaps because those categories are descriptively inadequate to the lived realities they purport to represent' (Gupta 1995: 384).

As these examples show, there are many problems in choosing a definition. Therefore, I do not attempt to do so. Instead, I will have a look at how Indian players talk about and use the concept of corruption in their quest for power and resources controlled by the state. In Northern India, the Hindi word 'brashtachaar' is used to refer to corruption. It refers to behaviour that is either illegal, violates social norms or is met with moral disapproval (Gupta 2005: 7). As Gupta summarised:

> '[E]xpectations of 'right' behavior, standards of accountability, and norms of conduct for state officials ... come from social groups as well as from 'the state'. Sometimes these standards and norms converge; more often, they do not. Thus, there are always divergent and conflic-

ting assessments of whether a particular course of action is 'corrupt'. Subjects' deployment of disourses of corruption are necessarily mediated by their structural location' (1995: 388).

For my study of corruption in India, I will keep in mind that the way in which a society (or an ethnographer or an author) evaluates a phenomenon such as corruption depends on socially shaped moral. A central question that remains to be answered with regard to corruption is thus whether there is a widely-shared agreement about exempting role incumbents of public office in India from the logic of short-term profit. Before looking at the Indian case to answer these questions, I will review some theories about corruption.

I.4. Approaches to the Study of Corruption

An abundance of literature has been written on the subject of corruption, most of which has not addressed the inherent ambiguity in defining the concept, but has treated this aspect as a non-issue. It would be a daunting task, and would lead to far in this context, to summarise all existing literature, but I will briefly look at three viewpoints from which the phenomenon of corruption has mostly been analysed: socio-cultural explanations, economic considerations and finally the legal and political point of view. I will attempt to demonstrate which ideas have influenced my way of looking at the phenomenon.

I.4.1. Socio-Cultural Explanations

Approaches widespread and popular until at least the 70s in particular, offered socio-cultural explanations of corruption. Corruption was seen as being endemic to the traditional, non-Western, underdeveloped, (one might add: irrational and ignorant) societies who were supposedly 'intrinsically caught in the webs of their culture' (Haller & Shore 2005: 3). Corruption in these societies was

> 'understood mainly in terms of the survival of traditional patterns of behaviour – communalism, clientelism ... and the like – into the era of modern politics and administration' (Theobald 1991: 80).

These approaches with their 'moral and evolutionary overtones', recalling 'the colonial discourse about the 'primitiveness' of 'savage societies' were often in development studies and media writings (Haller & Shore 2005: 3).

Recent dramatic corruption and fraud scandals, for example the ones connected to the US energy corporation Enron and the global telecommunications giant WorldCom uncovered in 2001 and 2002, have once again shattered the idea that corruption is only 'symptomatic of Third World instability' and does not have a place in stable Western states. The anthropologist Thomas Hauschild wrote in the German weekly 'Zeit' about corruption and patrimonialism under the German chancellor Helmut Kohl and concluded that:

> 'Ob in Neuguinea, Italien oder in der CDU – überall entdecken Ethnologen die gleichen Rituale ... Männerbünde, Gabentausch und Rituale der Macht' (Hauschild 2000)[6].

He suggested that there may be universal strategies related to exercising power, one of which is corruption. Theobald argues likewise that corruption and patrimonalism are universal phenomena which, 'manifest ... in ways that vary with specific social and economic backgrounds' (Theobald 1991: x).

In 1995, Hauschild and a team of anthropologists from Tübingen embarked on field research studying local-level clientelism after the Cold War in Italy and southern Germany. Observing big enterprises such as the construction of new bus terminals or streets or setting up new companies, the anthropologists witnessed how

> 'handfeste materielle Interessen zusammengingen mit altbewährten Strukturen des persönlichen Vertrauens' (Hauschild 2000)[7].

Hauschild reminds us that loyalty is essential for corrupt practices to flourish. When accomplices jointly break the law, they need to trust one another (Hauschildt 2000).

As early as 1977, anthropologist Eric Wolf argued that corruption and patrimonalism were prevalent in complex societies as side-arrangements that enabled the smooth functioning of the 'big' institutions (1977: 175). He confirmed his hypothesis when studying the centrally planned Russian economy which, as he concluded, could not have survived without the side-activities of planners and company leaders who illegally exchanged resources and spare parts and established their bonds of trust by feasting together. He and his colleagues jointly studied such informal 'arrangements' across the world. In Latin America, local leaders had acquired such a mastery of the 'game' that democracy and the courts lost their real power altogether (Hauschild 2000). Wolf predicted that once the balance between the 'big institutions', namely the US and the Soviet Union, changed, so would the informal arrangements that had accompanied them (Wolf 1977: 175-176), a subject already outlined in the previous chapter I.2.1.

---

[6] Translation: Whether in New Guinea, Italy or the party of the German Christian Democrats, anthropologists discover the same rituals: male cliques, gift exchanges and rituals of power.
[7] Translated: Material interests went hand in hand with established structures of personal trust.

Looking at the case studies, it seems reasonable to assume that corruption is a widely used strategy in the struggle for power and control over resources. Learning from Wolf, I will try not to isolate my study of contemporary corruption in India from the framework of developments within India and trends in the world of politics and economics.

I.4.2. Economic Considerations

Theobald argued that corruption in economically advanced countries was less visible, because it mainly occured in the private sector and at the apex of the state apparatus - where politicians and businessmen felt exposed and vulnerable and therefore tried to surround themselves with allies - but less in the sphere of routine administration (Theobald 1991: 46), where bureaucrats mostly had secure and reasonably paid jobs with well-defined areas of authority. In developing countries, on the other hand, unemployment was high and bureaucrats often had to sustain a network of relatives from their income.

Economically, in developing countries,

> 'scarcity is the keynote of social existence: scarcity of jobs, material goods, hospital beds, school places, housing, land, skill, spare parts, potable water – in fact scarcity of everything' (Theobald 1991: 82),

and the state cannot materially satisfy the demands citizen's thrust upon it during Independence movements (compare chapter III.2.3.d). Since many developing countries' foreign exchange income mainly stems from exporting one or two basic commodities, it is subject to market fluctuations in the world price. A lot of the foreign exchange income thus generated is in turn used to service foreign debts rather than spending it on the goods and important factors needed for industrial development.

> 'This means that enterprises must periodically close down for want of spare parts or raw materials; household necessities disappear from the markets because they can't be imported or produced locally; jobs generally disappear, but especially jobs in the public sector as the latter's already weak material base is particularly sensitive to the vicissitudes of economic life' (Theobald 1991: 82).

Due to a shortage of resources the state cannot provide its citizens with even a basic social security net, which makes them turn to other, older forms of cooperation in order to ensure a minimum amount of safety. In such a situation, who does not play along with 'familism, communalism, clientelism, friendship (and) gift-giving[8] ... runs the risk of losing the right to expect succour from his peers should he need it in the future. In an overall situation of scarcity and insecurity, of chronic inflation and sudden shortage, *such obligations are not to be taken lightly.*' (Theobald 1991: 80, my italics).

Nevertheless, the necessity of having an informal network to make up for perceived basic economic vulnerability is, as I suggest, often not the primary factor leading to corruption in developed countries, nor is it always an explanation for corruption in economically weaker states. Needs are partially social constructs, and when considering the reasons for bribe-taking, the organisational culture within which people operate and the social peer group come into focus. In a newspaper article on the Enron corruption scandal, the author Thomas Fischermann (2006) wrote about the organisational culture that put all employees under extreme pressure. The most aggressive dealers were awarded bonuses of millions of dollars, while every six months one in ten employees got fired for not having earned enough profits. Fischermann argues that it was these incentives and the organisational culture, which lead to high-risk investments that did not yield results. This was when employees started altering accounts.

There are people who blame consumerism and subsequent corruption on the monetarised 'Western' economic model. Fuller emphasised instead that money, far from being a new invention, had been minted by Indian rulers as early as the second century BC. Two millennia ago, money lending in India was so widespread that it attracted the attention of Hindu lawmakers (Fuller 1989: 43). His review of the traditional Indian economic Jajmani system, which had long been regarded as a prime example of a traditional economy not subject to market pressures, showed instead that during the Mughal period, for example, cultivation in India clearly responded to market demands (Habib 1963: 75-81, quoted after Fuller 1989: 46).

Furthermore, anthropological comparisons have shown that even in cultures without money, there is often a sphere, though mostly 'with circumscribed limits', within which impersonal, competitive, individual, acquisitive, and purely instrumental activities take place. It would be misleading to attribute this to a specific economic system alone. Plunder and exploitation, likewise, are hardly new phenomena.

---

[8] In the Bhilai Steel Plants (a public sector enterprise) in the Chattisgarh region in Madhya Pradesh, Parry's (2000: 45) informants distinguished ('in ascending order of moral culpability') between 'gifts' for maintaining social relations, 'commissions', a fixed rate percentage on the value of all contracts, and 'bribes', a negotiable amount for passing sub-standard goods. As other literature does not make such distinctions, this will not be valid for my paper.

Other authors have looked at whether corruption obstructs or supports economic growth. While some argue that corruption has a positive effect on development, because it enhances entrepreneurial abilities, assists capital formation, and allows the logic of the market to penetrate into 'transactions from which public controls attempt to exclude it', others like Theobald (1991: 116, 125) and Parry (2000: 28) argue that entrepreneurialism is stifled by corruption, collected capital from corrupt earnings is often not spent locally but saved abroad and, most importantly, corruption squanders scarce national resources. Haller and Shore (2005: 7) argue that the results of corruption are typically

> 'inflated contracts, distorted development priorities, increased exploitation and inequality and heightened uncertainty' (Theobald 1991: 125).

I do not wish to evaluate whether corruption indeed undermines economic development as correlate statistics suggest (Krastev 2003: 122) or whether it is vice versa. Rather, I am interested in learning how corruption affects common Indians and whether it does in fact lead to increased exploitation of the poor or, instead, strengthens their position by offering them informal access to resources they could otherwise not have gotten hold of. Yet, as Haller & Shore cautioned us, we should be careful not to romanticise corruption as a 'weapon of the poor' but keep in mind that, as E. Dougherty put it in a meeting in 2000:

> 'Often the poorest sector of the population, who has little monetary or social capital with which to negotiate deals, is unable to partake and benefit from these informal systems of exchange and gift-giving' (Haller & Shore 2005: 17).

I conclude that economic, social or political vulnerability can be part of the explanation for corrupt behaviour, especially in a situation of economic scarcity and uncertainty or in circumstances in which the state does not even guarantee a minimum amount of security for its citizens. In such a situation people may turn to other, older forms of cooperation such as gift-giving to ensure the survival as a member of the social group they want to belong to with all the status symbols required by this social group.

I.4.3. Legalistic & Political Approaches

Many recent books on corruption take a rather technical approach to the subject, they address the question of how to place incentives and disincentives and how to improve laws and procedures in order to avoid corruption, an approach that is being promoted, among others, under the name "National Integrity System" by the public interest organisation Transparency International. While the structures are probably important to observe, reducing the 'fight against corruption' to improvement of institutions alone might easily miss the point, because, as Randhir B. Jain and his colleague P. S. Bawa (2003: 9) point out in their report for Transparency International, political and administrative institutions as well as the media and civil society in India are already strong and independent to a great extent, though more remains to be done. In his novel 'A fine Balance' set in Mumbai (formerly Bombay), the author Rohinton Mistry reminds us that the problem is not that laws are not passed, but rather, that they are hardly implemented. Listening to the politician's speeches at the election rallies one of the characters in the book, Dukhi, remarks to his friends: 'There must be a lot of duplication in our country's laws. ... Every time there are elections, they talk of passing the same ones passed twenty years ago. Someone should remind them they need to apply the laws.' 'For politicians, passing laws is like passing water,' said Narayan. 'It all ends down the drain.' (Mistry 1995: 143).

Elite theory and the social worker Mukat Singh, whom I met in India while doing fieldwork, stated that public policy and action did 'not reflect the demands of the masses but the prevailing values of the elite'. Usually the elite stems mainly from the upper classes and through its position aquires an interest to preserve the organisation and the base on which their power rests (Fels 2005, Dye & Zeigler 2003: 2,4,13-14).

Democratic governance, in Dye and Zeigler's view, is distinguished from totalitarian rule mainly by the existence of autonomous, legitimate elites outside the government. But while pluralism holds that competition between different elites safeguards democracy, elite theory assumes that

> 'accommodation, rather than competition is the prevailing style of elite interaction: "You scratch my back, and I'll scratch yours"' (Dye & Zeigler 2003: 11-14).

Only politicians have to answer to the public in elections, other elites like business leaders, bureaucrats and journalists cannot be held accountable (Fels 2005, Dye & Zeigler 2003: 14). Thus Dye and Ziegler conclude that

> 'when elites abandon democratic principles or the masses lose confidence in elites, democracy is in peril' (2003: 15-17).

In their eyes, the only check on elites' behaviour is their own interest in preserving the system. To 'restore mass confidence', they periodically initiate reforms to stop the most outrageous types of abuse inflicted upon the system. But no reform leaves a net without holes (and possibly it is not even intended to do so) which is why changing rules may not result in restraining self-interested elites in the long run.

Like Theobald, many authors fear that corruption may seriously undermine citizens' faith in democratic politics:

> 'Far from promoting political development, corruption leads to serious political decay in that it weakens administrative capacity and undermines democracy, stability and national integration' (Theobald 1991: 125).

It is paradoxical, however, that corruption is seen as the biggest threat to democracy and the rule of law, while it is precisely 'the rule of law and the legal and rational bureaucracy that gave rise to the concept of corruption in the first place' (Haller & Shore, 2005: 7). Maybe the ideas of rational, disinterested professionals working for the benefit of 'the public' were simply unrealistic? Or they were nothing but an illusion created by the powerful to distract the masses? But now citizens expect this idea to be turned into reality and, failing that, become frustrated?

In my analysis, I will try to maintain a balance between looking at structures, institutions and rules for the incentives and disincentives they offer, remaining alert to the sometimes disguised interests of the different elites in- and outside the government and their numerous ways of formally – and informally – altering the system to their advantage. Furthermore, I will investigate what ideas the Indian state was based on and how these ideas 'get along' with (or change?) reality.

I.4.4. Why an Anthropology of Corruption

As shown above, many of the approaches to the study of corruption have been normative and quite specific and therefore limited in their approach. Some of the findings have been used by players such as the World Bank for their own ends. One argument for an anthropology of corruption is therefore that anthropologists have learned to be sceptical about social sciences and critically evaluate the role they play (Haller & Shore 2005: 10) as I have attempted to do in chapter I.2.5.

Corruption, and the study of it, has many differing and confusing aspects to it and cannot easily be classified. We may not be able to solve the riddle, but we can

> 'certainly learn a great deal about our world by interrogating the idea of corruption and exploring its many different manifestations' (Haller & Shore 2005: 9).

Wade pointed out that, since corruption is normally hidden from the public eye, a researcher 'obviously ... cannot work towards an understanding of the phenomena ... by the familiar methods of random sample, the formal interview, and structured questionnaire. One has to use, rather more informal, more 'anthropological' means' (1982: 291).

Furthermore, rather than being concerned with theory-building and the analysis of abstract laws and institutions, anthropologists try to approach a subject by looking at it from the emic perspectives of those who experience corruption and putting it into a wider, holistic framework. What does it mean to them? What rules, norms and ideas govern their behaviour? What interests and struggles are hidden behind abstract definitions?

'Corruption is a form of exchange, a polysemous and multi-stranded relationship and part of the way in which individuals connect with the state',

summarise Haller and Shore (2005: 6-7). We pay attention to it because it matters to our informants, in fact, in almost every part of the world, common people, the media, and institutions have become fascinated with the phenomenon. Visvanathan and Sethi stressed in 1998 that to understand corruption, we have to cast off our puritan bias and instead look at it as if it were 'a ritual'. Following him, Haller and Shore (2005: 6-7) conclude that we have to grasp 'both the politics and the poetics of corruption, to gain the measure of its cultural complexity.'

In this paper, I will try to see what we can learn and what hypothesis' can be generated from looking at ethnographies about corruption in India.

To start off, I will shortly look at the performance of the independent Indian state in those areas vital to its legitimacy: democracy, development, and public welfare, since this is the background against which the harm caused by corruption is measured. As Gupta stated

'the postcolonial state has itself generated new discourses of accountability. Actions tolerated or considered legitimate under colonial rule may be classified as 'corrupt' by the rule-making apparatuses of the independent nation-state because an electoral democracy is deemed accountable to 'the people'' (1995: 388).

II. Setting: The Indian State

II.1. Ideas of India

The Indian state was first imagined by outsiders. Before the British ruled the subcontinent, no emperor had ever controlled the whole territory which holds today the world's largest democracy. Bawa and Jain (2003: 16) commented that,

'India inherited a legacy of corruption from its ancient rulers who always expected some gifts ... from their subjects. Appointments to the key positions were made on family considerations... Thus, nepotism ... was an acceptable concept. ... Corruption in India is also a legacy of the colonial system. As colonial governments were generally regarded as alien and hence illegitimate, consequently cheating and deceiving such an alien power was considered a fair game. ... The cheating of foreign rulers in government came to be admired as a patriotic virtue.'

In opposition to the British rulers, people belonging to a multitude of different language groups, communities and religions came to define themselves as Indian (Khilnani 2004: 18). India became one of the first truly multicultural democratic states.

II.1.1. Social & Economic Development

The exploitation of India's resources by the British, as the 'drain theory' had spelled out, was one of the strongest arguments of the Independence movement (Corbridge & Harris 2000: 14; Khilnani 2004: 68-69). After the withdrawal of the colonialists, many expected wealth would come to the Indians and poverty would diminish (Khilnani 2004: 65). Nehru saw the eradication of poverty through developmental measures as the most important task for the new indigenous government. As in most post-colonial countries, the goal was to achieve economic development in order to abolish the material poverty of the masses. Harris and Corbridge (2000: xvii) neatly summed it up as follows:

'The whole enterprise of 'development' ... owed a great deal to the arguments within the Indian nationalist movement and in the Constituent Assembly. Development was the *raison d'etre* of the modern state and the source of its legitimacy.'

II.1.2. Politics - Democracy in Diversity

The choice of democracy for the newly formed country (made not by the masses, but by the governing intellectual elite) was less obvious - and clearly in contrast to the paths chosen by many other independent new states (Khilnani 2004: 9, 29, 34). Democracy in a multicultural country such as India with looming social and economic inequalities was clearly an experiment (Khilnani 2004: 16), and a contradictory one, too, as Ambedkar, the leader of the Indian Untouchables foresaw in 1949:

> 'On the 26th of January 1950, we are going to enter a life of contradictions. In politics we will have equality and in social and economic life we will have inequality. ... How long shall we continue to live this life of contradictions? How long shall we continue to deny equality in our social and economic life? If we continue to deny it for long, we do so only by putting our political democracy in peril' (after Khilnani 2004: 35).

Similarly, Samuel Huntington warned in 1968 that pursuing development and democracy at the same time might lead to contradictions, because economic development without adequate redistribution would lead to more social inequality and could thus, instead of leading to stability and democracy, undermine the public order. He forecast that social mobilisation would lead to 'mounting pressure on the state to meet mass demands, demands for jobs, hospitals, schools, roads, electricity, and the like.' Since governmental institutions were (financially) ill-equipped to deal with these demands, he concluded that 'Political modernisation, that is mobilisation, [might] lead to political decay' (quoted after Theobald 1991: 77).

II.2. Performance of Democracy

Looking at the performance of the Indian state nearly sixty years later, an evaluation of its achievements and failures is not an easy task. Democracy, to the surprise of many sceptics, has survived and is indeed vital. According to Khilnani, it is also today at the heart of the Indian imagination, where it has 'begun to corrode the authority of the social order and of a paternalist state' (Khilnani, 2004: 17). More groups than ever before try to play an active part in shaping their own future (Khilnani 2004: 13). The story of the political rise of the Scheduled Castes and Tribes and the Other Backward Classes, as they have been labelled by the Indian government for reservationist purposes[9], has given the Indian lower classes some self-esteem and power and a (though still limited) greater measure of independence from the

---

[9] 'Affirmative Action': In order to give disadvantaged groups and castes the opportunity to share in the benefits the new state had to offer, quotas were successfully reserved for the so-called 'Scheduled Castes and Tribes' (SC/ST) (Corbridge & Harris 2000: 210) and later on also for 'Backward' and 'Other Backward Classes' (OBC) for example in government jobs and educational facilities. A more sombre note, this has given rise to modern forms of political communalism and casteism (Khilnani 2004: 36-37, 57).

dominant social groups (Corbridge & Harris 2000: 208-209; Khilnani 2004: 10). Politics have turned chaotic as new groups like rich farmers and lower castes have entered and made their claims on resources controlled by the state, as Huntington had foreseen (see previous page).

'The steady political mobilization [brought] lower and poorer people into politics, many who were organizing themselves into groups defined by legally ascribed identities. The Backward and Other Backward Classes, the Scheduled Castes and others' (Khilnani 2004: 181).

Electoral populism introduced by Indira Gandhi and today used by most politicians appeals directly to the Indian electorate, especially those communal groups which are numerically strong (Khilnani 2003: 44-49). Populist appeals to communalism and the violence they produce are judged by some to be the biggest immediate threat to the survival of the multicultural democracy (Khilnani 2004: xiii-xv, Hansen 2001: 31-67). According to Khilnani, the 'violence that began to seep into public life was expressive of conflicts related to the rising levels of democratic participation' (Khilnani 2004: 49). Others are afraid that the discrepancy between promises and performance of corrupt politicians may lead citizens to lose faith in democratic institutions which are supposed to be impartial and benevolent (Vittal 2003: 14-17, Kashyap 2001: VII, Singh 2001: 8, Parry 2000: 28). Corbridge and Harris as well as Khilnani reject this idea, because in a 'national study conducted in 1996, more than 70 percent of the electorate rejected the idea that India would be better governed without political parties and elections' (Khilnani 2004: 58). This shows that Indians are indeed deeply committed to (and realistic in their expectations of) the imperfect democracy they live in, which, though disappointing in many ways, has also unevenly opened up new space for empowerment (Corbridge & Harris 2000: xix, 202, for further elaboration compare chapter III.3). Anyhow, as Jayal (2001(1): 98) pointed out, although

'traditionally deprived communities were empowered by a new consciousness of their rights, their demands for economic redistribution were not met. ... The response of the state to the problems of poverty, unemployment and vast disparities of wealth, and to pressures for an all-providing state, took [only] the form of populist politics.'

This is why economic development and what it has delivered to the citizens of India will be examined more closely in the following part of my paper.

II.3. Performance of Economic Development

On the economic front, the overall comparative evaluation is less positive. Khilnani (2004: 62) sums it up as follows:

> 'The economy created in the name of the intellectual blueprint of the 1950s, founded on heavy industry and isolated from international competition, has not delivered its promises.'

Since the 1980s India has achieved considerable growth, making it 'one of the most rapidly growing economies in the world in the 1990s' (Murgai et al. 2006: 2) (starting from an extremely low base, of course). Still, the new wealth generated has hardly been distributed evenly. Some numbers illustrating the overall developmental achievements – and failures[10]: between 1951 and 2000 the production of food has grown fourfold. The life expectancy has also doubled, to 63 years at present, and the rate of infant death has fallen by more than fifty percent. Nevertheless, measured by the head-count index of poverty, 36.6 percent of the rural and 19 percent of the urban Indian population still lived in poverty in 1998 (Drèze & Sen 2006: 409-411). Nearly three fourths of the poor reside in rural areas (Murgai et al. 2006: 22). The poverty figures, which began to fall only after 1983, are today significantly lower than in 1951 (36.1 and 45.6 percent, respectively), but since the population has grown so fast (by two percent on annual average), the absolute number of the poor has even increased. Between 1951 and 2001 the number of those who can read has more than tripled, but forty percent of all Indians are still illiterate, especially women (Drèze & Sen 2006: 409-411). Even among the middle-income group more than half of all children are still underweight, especially girls (Murgai et al. 2006: 11-12).

The reasons for the economic successes and failures are essentially political (Parry 2000: 27, Khilnani 2004: 10) and home-made (Khilnani 2004: 63):

> 'The basic dilemma of independent India's pursuit of economic development was in a country where the great weight of numbers as well as considerable wealth, lay in the countryside, there were relative few pressures to industrialize, still less to redistribute or to effect social reforms' (Khilnani 2004: 75).

Because of the absence of private initiative or capital, the government focused on building an industrial sector, neglecting redistributional measures. After Independence, it tried harder to raise the level of production than to achieve a more equal distribution of wealth. State-owned companies and

---

[10] The aggregate numbers conceal wide, sometimes dramatic, regional disparities (Murgai et al 2006: 24), which cannot be discussed here. See chapter III for a very short discussion.

industry were supported, but small-scale enterprises, in which poor people tend to work, were not given equal importance. The 'Green Revolution' introduced new farming techniques and was successful in achieving higher yields, but it was mainly middle-class peasants who benefitted, because they had enough money to invest in costly equipment in the first place. New health centres and educational facilities were built, but mostly in cities not for the majority of the poor Indian peasants. There was more investment in higher educational facilities, less in primary schools (Kumar, 1997: 6).

II.3.1. Industry & Protectionism

In order to safeguard the emerging indigenous industry from outside pressures, Nehru and his companions financed it with state resources and protected it from international competition by extensive bureaucratic controls as well as 'inward-looking trade and foreign investment policies'. Today, the performance of many public sector enterprises is miserable, because in the absence of outer pressures or internal incentives, efficiency remained abysmally low:

> 'The result was a 'control-infested system' that smothered private initiative and encouraged the proliferation of inefficiencies and corruption, within both the state-controlled economy and the political system as a whole' (Khilnani 2004: 97).

Loss-making public enterprises remain a constant drain on the resources of the state as governments continue to support them (as well as big private companies in danger of going bankrupt) for fear of massive social unrest if it closed them down and sent large numbers of workers, who have to support their families, into unemployment (and poverty, as there is no social security – Matter 1999: 2, Khilnani 2004: 91-92). The tariffs and duties intended to protect the Indian market became – in the absence of profitable public enterprises or an effective income tax[11] – the one most important income generating instrument for the Indian state. Khilnani's (2004: 96) conclusion of the effects of protectionism:

> 'The profusion of controls had failed to create a productive public sector, squeezed out private enterprise, and given the state access to resources used not for welfare but as pools of patronage.'

---

[11] Two percent of India's urban population pay income tax and 'the economic reforms have continued to evade the issue of taxing agricultural wealth and incomes' (Khilnani 2004: 103).

II.3.2. Peasants & Land Redistribution

As in many other parts of the world, most of the Indian poor live in rural areas. In 1994, sixty-seven percent of all Indians worked in the agricultural sector which was then responsible for twenty-nine percent of the Gross National Product (Harris-White 2004: 19). One of the reasons for the peasants' poverty is the unequal ownership of land. In 1992-3, thirty-six percent of village inhabitants did not own land (Drèze & Sen 2006: 404), and in 1995 approximately five million peasants still worked for years without being paid, because they were indebted.

In the fifties and sixties, several regional governments tried to redistribute the land to achieve higher productivity and a more equal distribution of wealth, but these attempts often failed[12], because many landlords 'redistributed' 'their land'[13] only to relatives and friends. (Hörig, 1995: 31-57, Khilnani 2004: 78-79). Nevertheless, particularly in places with absentee landlords, there was a significant reallocation of land rights. In general, large landlords and small tenants were the losers and the middle levels, both landlords and tenants, gained. A second agricultural improvement of the 1950s was the increase in area under irrigation (Robinson 1988: 5).

Small-scale agriculture in India had long suffered from low levels of investment because of the zamindari system:

> High rents, high rates of interest and low prices [left] the mass off petty peasants with very little to invest in the development of the land, and [kept] them at the mercy of the more powerful in the village' (Thorner and Thorner 1962: 3, quoted after Corbridge & Harris 2000: 11).

Thus, when Independence came, Indian agriculture had a very low productivity (Khilnani 2004: 78-79). The immediate benefits of the Green Revolution mainly went to middle-class peasants in Northern India, mostly in Punjab.[14] The British colonial government supported monocultures and

---

[12] With the notable exception of Kerala (and later West Bengal), where freely elected Communist governments achieved remarkable results. Kerala, however, had a much more equal distribution of land to begin with (Khilnani 2002: 79).

[13] The land that given to them by the British, who had often 'assigned ownership to local grandees in return for rents paid to the 'Company Raj' (Khilnani 2003: 66).

[14] Which is not to deny that the rest of the population may benefit indirectly from the availability of greater quantities of food on the market which leads to lower prices (thus, of course, also diminishing profits for marginal farmers who could not equally raise their productivity). In the village Palanpur in Uttar Pradesh, even smaller farmers directly benefitted from the Green Revolution, because the ownership of land was less concentrated than in other areas (Drèze, Lanjouw & Sharma 1998: 228).

big plantations in order to raise a modern, more productive, commercialised agriculture. Many small peasants, mostly from lower castes, lost their land (Hörig 1995: 61-65). This is just one illustration of the contradictions that can arise between the two stated goals of development and democracy (as Huntington had warned, compare chapter 2.1.2.) in India. Mitra explained that, like the British, whose developmental agenda it inherited,

> 'the post-colonial state was caught in a paradox where its democratic credentials required it to turn to the society for political support and legitimacy, whereas its agenda of development and nation-building involved the destruction of the customary rights and parochial ways of parts of the society' (Mitra 1992: 5).

II.3.3. Economic Populism & Liberalisation

The same paradox can emerge between popular demands and reasonable economic development in the modern sector, as the 1960s showed. Indira Gandhi, then prime minister, responded to the claims of various newly-risen groups by nationalising sick enterprises to save jobs (thus bloating the public sector), giving subsidies for electricity, water, fertilisers and credit to prosperous peasants (in order to do so, she had to nationalise the banks), while leaving agricultural incomes and wealth untaxed and giving nothing but vague and ultimately empty promises of redistribution to the poor (Khilnani 2004: 91-92).[15]

The fiscal crisis in the 1990s, caused among other factors by this excessive government spending as well as rising interest rates on the international market, forced the government to ask the International Monetary Fund for one of its concessional loans (Khilnani 2004: 94-95). Therefore, some of the subsidies for the peasants as well as protectionist measures had to be reduced. Yet, six years later, the reforms have not caused a major shift in many important areas:

---

[15] This, however, is Khilnani's evaluation. Robinson disagrees. She argues that although Indira Gandhi (during the Emergency that she had declared from 1975 to 1977) jailed her political opponents, suspended political bodies, thus giving new power to bureaucrats, altered the Constitution, restricted the press and had the sterilisation programme implemented by using threats of force, the economic position of some of the marginalised citizens was improved at the same time due to several reasons: Land ceiling laws were widley publicised and sometimes implemented, an attempt was made to release bonded labour, village banks were established and loans without collateral were given to curb the power of local moneylenders. Some tax evaders were arrested, which undermined corrupt local power strcutures, and increased productivity was achieved by electrification and irrigation (Robinson 1988: 194).

'government borrowing remained high, most of it being used to subsidise and placate, and not for productive or infrastructural purposes … and in the face of trade union resistance, there was no move to privatize public enterprises … If anything, liberalization seemed to nourish still more magnificent scales of corruption: mutually beneficial transactions in the stock exchange and in the sugar, power and telecommunications industries left the wardrobes of cabinet ministers bursting with cash...' (Khilnani 2004: 99).

Due to pressures from the World Trade Organisation, India has, in the interest of its industrial elite, recently significantly lowered the tarrifs meant to protect the internal market. Especially small farmers have been hit hard by these measures. After years of low levels of investment, due to exploitation by the landlords, and guaranteed prices for fertilisers as well as for the produce which were set by the state, they now suddenly have to compete with subsidised products from the US and the European Union. Naturally, they could not prevail. The prices for fertilisers exploded, while the prices for their produce fell so much, that farmers today are again deeply indebted to local moneylenders and desperate. Prices for processed products, cotton for example, remain however high. The whole profit goes to middlemen. Additionally, levels of groundwater have fallen in regions with intensified agriculture and soils are often drained due to heavy use of fertilisers. The peasants' situation is so disastrous that, statistically speaking, in only one single province (Vidarbha) in the state of Maharashtra in Northern India, every eight hours an Indian farmer commits suicide, because he does not see any other solution (Schmitt 2006).

There have been numerous protests against this process of liberalisation initiated since 1991, often by farmer's organisations, which I cannot summarise nor evaluate here in detail. Anyhow, one point is still worth noting: Sen and Drèze argue that the public preoccupation with the issue of liberalisation has led the public to neglect more fundamental issues of structural social inequalities and basic deprivations for a majority of the poor. Due to the significance of their argument, I will quote it at length:

> 'We believe that the concentration on defending or attacking liberalization as the central policy issue distracts attention from a broader understanding of social opportunities. … The central issue, we have argued, is to expand the social opportunities open to the people. In so far as these opportunities are compromised – directly or indirectly – by counterproductive regulations and controls, by restrictions on economic initiatives, by the stifling of competition and its efficiency-generating advantages, and so on, the removal of these hindrances must be seen as extremely important … [But] while the case for

economic reforms may take good note of the diagnosis that India has too much government in some areas, it ignores the fact that India also has *insufficient and ineffective government activity in many other areas*, including school education, health care, social security, land reform, environmental protection and the promotion of social change. This inertia, too, contributes to the persistence of widespread deprivation and social inequality (Drèze & Sen 2006: 345-346, my italics).

The importance as well as the – often disastrous – performance of these basic state services will be examined more in detail in chapter II.4.

II.3.4. Access to Natural Resources

As there is a scarcity of reasonably paid jobs in India, many of those who are most marginalised, agricultural workers, small farmers and 70 million Adivasis, the biggest indigenous population in the world, still depend not only on subsistence agriculture, but also on resources from the commons, such as the forests (Hörig 1995: 86). Gadgil and Guha called those Indians who depended on natural resources for their means of survival the 'ecosystem people' and argued that they made up about fifty percent of India's population. Another third of the population, according to their estimates, have become 'ecological refugees' because of environmental degradation and pollution. Thus a social minority 'develops' and profits at the cost of nature and the social majority (after Corbridge & Harris 2000: 207). In a symposium held in 2004, Shiva and Sachs argued that whereas there had always been Indians with few possessions, before 'development' came about, many of these Indians were at least able to survive in a frugal, yet dignified manner, because they had access to the commons such as land and water (Fels 2004). Shiva challenged the theory of the 'Tragedy of the Commons' and instead, asserted, as studies in Pakistan and North India have also shown (Kreutzmann 1990: 10-23, Guha 1989: 28-33, Tewari 1995: 138-139), that the use of the commons had often been regulated by local communities so as to preserve them for the future. In the course of development, the commons had been appropriated by the colonial government, a legacy not revised by the indigenous government after 1947. The forest, for example, is today used for state development projects, and trees are cut down for ever-more agricultural land to feed India's growing population. Natural forests are often replaced by commercial monocultures of teak or eucalyptus for export (to generate the foreign exchange income needed to pay for imports and to service foreign debts). Every year 1.5 million hectares of forest are lost in India. This leads to floods, erosion and draughts in the valleys, because the forest is lost as a water storage (Hörig 1995: 88-97). It is also a disaster for some of the Adivasi communities like the Van Gujjar I visited in Uttaranchal, as they live in and from the forest. Their homes are being destroyed through mining, dams and industry or they are declared National Parks as the West defines them: places where people are not permitted to live. The displaced Adivasi have to fight for survival as agricultural labourers who posess hardly any rights, or in urban squatter settlements.

II.3.5. Livelihoods in the Unregistered Sector

The majority of Indians today work in the vast unregistered sector which includes agriculture as well as informal and black market activities. The term 'informal' is misleading, as many of these market activities are in fact very well organised. Only seven percent of all Indians, the privileged upper class, work in the formal, registered sector and enjoy the benefits of unions and state protection. Their wealth depends in no small part on the negligible cost of casual labour. Those who work in the unregistered sector lack the enforcement of minimum wages as well as labour protection laws, such as measures against child labour or working conditions causing health hazards. Many of them view the state as a distant legislator neglecting to implement the measures intended for their protection (Harris-White 2004: 17-9). Drèze, Lanjouw and Sharma (1998: 226), talking about a small village in Northern India which was examined in detail by economists over several decades since Independence, remarked:

> 'There [were] ... plenty of official rules purporting to regulate labour transactions, tenancy agreements, credit contracts, marketing arrangements, and even food trade. For better or worse, however, most of these official rules ha[d] little force in practice. In fact, it can be argued that Palanpur [was] already a highly liberalized economy, a kind of Chicago economists' paradise where an effectively unregulated market exist[ed] for almost everything. ... The notion that further liberalization [could be] the key to rapid and equitable development is wishful thinking.'

II.4. Welfare State? – Selected Public Services

After Independence, it soon became clear that the benefits of economic development did not, as had been expected, automatically 'trickle down' to the poor (van Kampen 2000: 8). Thus in 1972, the Indian government decided to 'provide and improve basic amenities, mainly in the rural areas' to attack poverty directly (van Kampen 2000: 202). From then on, at least ideologically, 'India's Development has been based on a two-pronged approach: accelerated economic growth and redistribution for social development'. The performance of the adopted economic strategies and the most important consequences have been sketched above. This chapter is concerned with the performance of selected public institutions and development schemes. In 1947, Nehru stated in the Constituent Assembly:

> 'The first task of this Assembly is to free India through a new constitution, to feed the starving people, and to clothe the naked masses, and give every Indian the fullest opportunity to develop himself according to his capacity' (after Corbridge & Harris 2000: 20).

Some of the reasons why economic development did not lead to the desired eradication of poverty, have been discussed above. This chapter focuses on those public institutions vital for extending citizens' opportunities in a modern democratic state with a free market economy. First, I will focus on educational facilities and their performance. As will be evident from the case studies discussed below, literacy is vital for social mobility as well as for empowerment in a modern state depending to a great extent on formalised procedures (Drèze & Sen 2006: 143). In part II.4.1 I will discuss the performance of primary schools in India. Following this section, I will talk about the performance of health care centres, because a fundamental prerequisite for participation in political and economic life is physical well-being. In India, however, malnutrition and preventable diseases remain widespread (Drèze & Sen 2006: 196, 201), both as a result of poverty (adressed above) and the poor performance of public institutions which will be discussed in section II.4.2 In the following chapter, II.4.3, I will talk about the Indian state's development schemes, some of which will be presented in more detail in the case studies discussed in the third part of my paper.

II.4.1. Educational Facilities

Drèze and Sen (2006: 143), discussing the importance of education for all citizens, made an important point when summarising:

> 'An illiterate person is significantly less equipped to defend herself in court, to obtain a bank loan, to enforce her inheritance rights, to take advantage of new technology, to compete for secure employment, to get on the right bus, to take part in political activity – in short, to participate successfully in the modern economy and society.'

In 2001, seventy-six percent of the male Indian population (seven years and older) could read and write, but only fifty-four percent of the females (Drèze & Sen 2006: 410). As school attendance among the younger age group is a good indicator of trends in literacy, it is a good sign that almost eighty percent of the children in the six to fourteen age group go to school today. It is also noteworthy that seventy-four percent of all girls this age attend school, which shows that the earlier gender gap is decreasing (Drèze & Sen 2006: 151). Infrastructure has also improved: In 1993, about ninety-four percent of the rural population lived within one kilometre of a primary school (Drèze & Sen 2006: 166). While the trends point the right way, much remains to be done. A recent survey,

> 'the PROBE survey, found that there was no teaching activity whatsoever in half of the sample schools at the time of the investigator's (unannounced) visit. Overcrowded classrooms, a crumbling infrastructure, absence of teaching aids and dull teaching methods also undermined the quality of schooling. Pupil achievements were abysmally low, with, for instance, many children unable to read or write even after several years of schooling. In light of these survey findings, it is not surprising that parents often lose patience with government schools, even when they have a genuine interest in education' (Drèze & Sen 2006: 158).

Because of the bad quality of teaching in government schools, parents prefer to send their children to private schools, 'even though this usually means paying the full cost of education themselves' (Murgai et al. 2006: 16). Poorer parents, too, often make great monetary sacrifices to send their children to private institutions, especially in urban areas, where they are readily accessible. In the urban areas of five Indian states almost two thirds of the enrolled children go to private schools (Murgai et al. 2006: 16), leaving the public schools to those who are already economically marginalised. The educational gap widens, because public institutions do not work as they should and – other than in speeches – the national government seems to lack real commitment to universal elementary education, as can be seen from budget expenditures. Even though all major parties promised in their election manifestoes to raise public expenditure for education to six percent of GDP, the ratio has in fact declined in the nineties under successive governments, from 4.4 percent in 1989 to approximately 3.6 percent towards the end of the decade (Drèze & Sen 2006: 166). But there are informative regional differences. In spite of a rather slow growth compared with other states, Kerala, for example, invested much more in educational facilities[16] (Kumar, 1997: 1-8) with visible success: In 2001, ninety-four percent of its men and eighty-eight percent of the women could read and write (Drèze & Sen 2006: 393).

A common finding of village studies as well as household surveys is that parents are eager to educate their children, as literacy is seen as the most promising means for upward mobility (Drèze & Sen 2006: 144), Drèze and Sen (2006: 159) conclude that

---

[16] As did Himachal Pradesh, which is an even more astonishing example, because it did not, as Kerala, have a long history of education to look back on (see Drèze & Sen 2006: 177-186).

'there is every reason to expect parents and children to respond positively to public initiatives aimed at facilitating their involvement in the schooling system. That expectation is amply confirmed by recent experiences, from the striking popularity of many schools run by non-government organizations among disadvantaged communities to the overwhelming response to Madhya Pradesh's 'education guarantee scheme'. The effectiveness of these initiatives reflect the fact that much can be done without delay to overcome the 'discouragement effect': improving the accessibility of schools, organizing enrolment drives, providing school meals, upgrading the infrastructure, raising pupil-teacher ratios, supplying free textbooks, improving teacher supervision, making the curriculum and classroom processes more child-friendly, to cite a few examples. There is, in short, enormous scope for rapid progress towards universal elementary education'.

II.4.2. Health Care

There is a similar situation with regard to health care in India. In terms of expenditure, India has one of the six most 'privatised' health systems in the world. Despite official rhetoric, and only as a result of public institutions' poor performance (Murgai et al. 2006: 15). The Indian state only spends approximately 0.8 percent of GDP on health care facilities, further diminished 'by a highly inefficient use of available resources' (Drèze & Sen 2006: 202). Again, notwithstanding the fact that the infrastructure has been improved, the quality of the services has not:

> 'In many states, health centres are dilapidated, medicines are not available, doctors are chronically absent, and patients are routinely charged for services meant to be free (when they are treated at all). ... The dismal state of public health services is the main reason why most patients turn to private providers, however unreliable or expensive' (Drèze & Sen 2006: 206).

Private health care centres are in practice hardly regulated, in part because of their often informal nature, but also because of widespread corruption (Drèze & Sen 2006: 206). A recent survey in Rajasthan found that while the better-off cope with the inadequate performance of public facilities by visiting private doctors, the poor tend to visit health care centres less often (Murgai et al. 2006: 15). As a consequence, many preventable illnesses like tetanus, measles, pneumonia, leprosy, malaria, hepatitis and tuberculosis, which have sharply declined in other parts of the developing world, are still very common in India. For example, India's share of worldwide leprosy is estimated to be as high as sixty-eight percent. Likewise, nutrition-related ailments are very widespread judged by international standards. Malnutrition, too, is still a common consequence of poverty. The situation of girls and women is generally worse than that of males (Drèze & Sen 2006: 201). Yet public health services are not equally disastrous all over India. In some regions and especially in states like Kerala, Tamil Nadu, Gujarat and Maharashtra, where public services are generally more effective, health facilities seem to provide useful and reasonably equitable services (Drèze & Sen 2006: 207). In Kerala, the effects are again impressive: In 1993-7, the life expectancy of Keralan women was seventy-six years, nineteen years more than in Uttar Pradesh and the fertility rate was only 1.8 percent in 1996-8 (still 3.1% for all of India in 1999 – Drèze & Sen 2006: 393). This is why the absolute number of the poor is also declining in Kerala: In 1994 there were only half as many poor citizens as in 1974 (Kumar, 1997: 1-8).

II.4.3. Development Programmes

Since the seventies, the Indian state has introduced 'large-scale, and often nation wide, anti-poverty programmes' (van Kampen 2000: 8-9) to improve literacy and health (for example by organising immunisation camps), to provide certain commodities at subsidised prices (in ration shops), to make affordable credit accessible to the poor, to support cooperatives, to improve rural infrastructure (streets, water and electricity), to provide housing to the poor, to provide widows' and old-age pensions or to provide employment opportunities etc. (Drèze, Lanjouw & Sharma 1998 (1): 180 ff). Van Kampen (2000: 8) says these plans are generally well thought out, but their implementation has been much criticised. However, although 'a certain amount of government inertia, corruption, and inefficiency can be found everywhere in the country', there are, again, wide regional disparities. States like Kerala have steadily improved the performance of their public services (Drèze, Lanjouw & Sharma 1998 (1): 208). To name just one example: In 1986-7, eighty-eight percent of the citizens in Kerala received food grains from the public distribution system, sixty-nine kilogrammes per capita each year. In Uttar Pradesh, where poverty is much more widespread, only two percent of the rural population received subsidised food grains, amounting to no more than three kilogrammes each year per head (Drèze, Lanjouw & Sharma 1998 (1): 209). Several reasons for programme failures in weaker regions have been cited, including weak programme targeting, poor target group participation, political pressures and top-down, bureaucratic decision-making. Some blame the failure mainly on the deterioration of the political system and corruption and insist that there is an urgent need to change the current culture within the administration, which is based on individual self-interest and concentration of power and knowledge (van Kampen 2000: 8-9). There are too many programmes to list, but a few schemes will be introduced in the ethnographic case studies of corruption.

II.4.4. Conclusion: The State of Public Services

After Independence, the indigenous government had to legitimate its authority by providing for the welfare and freedom of its citizens (Khilnani 2004: 33). Thus, under its first prime minister, Nehru, the Indian

> 'state was enlarged, its ambitions inflated, and it was transformed from a distant, alien object into one that aspired to infiltrate the everyday lives of Indians, proclaiming itself responsible for everything they could desire: jobs, ration cards, educational places, security, cultural recognition' (Khilnani 2004: 41).

Yet, poor implementation of government plans is a major problem in many Indian regions today. Disappointed citizens thus become 'deeply alienated by the very programmes that the state [employs] to legitimate its rule' (Gupta 1995: 383). Faced with the poor performance of public institutions, many Indians have to turn to the private sector to satisfy fundamental needs such as health care and education (Murgai et al. 2006: 11-12). Even though there are numerous development schemes especially designed for the benefit of marginalised citizens and regions, many of them are dysfunctional. As the World Bank summarises

> 'Faced with inadequate public services, both elites and non-elites have developed ways to augment education, water, and health services in the private sector. ... a striking feature of the recent Indian experience is ... a completely ad hoc, unregulated privatization of services because of a systemic failure in the accountability of public sector for the quality of services' (Murgai et al. 2006: 11).

Looking at the failure of development projects in Lesotho, Ferguson (1990: 255) asked, 'if it is true that 'failure' is the norm of development projects' then what is the logic behind it? His conclusion:

> 'the 'development' apparatus in Lesotho is not a machine for eliminating poverty ... it is a machine for reinforcing and expanding the exercise of bureaucratic state power, which incidentally takes 'poverty' as its point of entry.'

In India, however, it would be false to say that public services never work, according to what regional differences in performance suggest. Rather, the factors leading to the differences must be investigated more closely. In the following ethnographic part of my paper I will focus on the role and influence of, as well as on the relations and dependencies between, marginalised citizens, bureaucrats and politicians, as other factors (like, for instance, institutional constraints, lawmaking or economic aspects) have already been given a great deal of attention in the literature (see chapter I.4).

III. Making Sense of Corruption in India

In this third and main part of my paper I would like to look at how corruption is experienced and interpreted by certain sample Indian players from more marginalised sections of society, from the bureaucracy and from politics. The main question I attempt to answer is how they experience and deal with corruption and – as far as this is discernible – what attitude towards the state arises or may arise from these experiences.

In the section on marginalised citizens, I will focus on strategies of resistance against exploitation employed by different players, and on the role of information. In the second part on bureaucrats, who often take bribes form citizens, I will investigate how and under which pressures officials operate. I will also address performative aspects involved in bribe-giving. In the third section, I will discuss the role of political players. Here, I will investigate local power configurations, economic dependencies, and accountability.

In each of the sections, I will first present three case studies which look at the central players from several angles and in varying circumstances. I will discuss my findings in summary in the second part of each section. There I will also make use of insights from other case studies and further literature. I have chosen this sequence to separate the more descriptive summaries from my interpretation, in order to give the reader the opportunity to get an 'impression' of what corruption looks (and might 'feel') like in India, before taking him to the more abstract level of generalisations.

As already mentioned in the outline (chapter I.1), most of my case studies are from more or less impoverished rural areas in different regions of India, namely in Uttar Pradesh, Rajasthan, South India (not specified), Andhra Pradesh, Bihar and West Bengal. While there are wide regional disparities in levels of poverty and development, 'correcting for cost-of-living differences across states, the large differences across people within rich states implies that the poorer sections of more wealthy states are very nearly as poor as those in poorer states' (Murgai et al. 2006: 24-6).

Although the range of people's encounters with the state is vast – they interact, for example, regularly with schools, health care centres and the police – my paper focuses principally on developmental institutions and schemes, because it is about this area of the state that I found some useful literature which focused at least in part on corruption.

III.1. Marginalised Citizens & Resistance

III.1.1. Citizens & Corruption: Case Studies

What does corruption look like for those at the base of society, those who should benefit from government programmes? How do the supposed benefactors perceive and interact with 'the state'? The three case studies examine corruption in North Indian villages and reveal answers to those questions.

In the first case study, a brief but comprehensive overview of public services and development schemes in Palanpur, a village in Uttar Pradesh, is given to get an idea of the local workings of the state in one specific village. The focus of the second, ethnographic case study is the attempt of a single low caste villager to benefit from a public housing scheme and the problems he encounters. In the final case study of this chapter, the attention is turned to a collective attempt at challenging structures of exploitation: I will introduce the Mazdoor Kisan Shakti Sangathan (MKSS), an organisation which initiated a social movement for the right to information in Rajasthan.

After summarising how citizens encounter corruption and deal with it, their attitude and reaction towards the state as well as their attempt to make sense of corrupt behaviour will be explored.

III.1.1.a. Public Services in Uttar Pradesh

Palanpur is a village in Moradabad District of western Uttar Pradesh with a population of 1,133 in 1993. The main economic activities are agriculture, livestock and employment outside the village. Ninety-six percent of the land under cultivation was irrigated, but only nine percent of the women and thirty-seven percent of the men were literate (Drèze & Sharma 1998: 14), compared to thirty-one and fifty-eight percent for all of rural India, respectively, in 1991 (Drèze & Sharma 1998: 24). Uttar Pradesh

> 'combines a high incidence of poverty ... with exceptionally high levels of mortality, fertility, undernutrition, illiteracy and related indicators of endemic deprivation. ... Uttar Pradesh is also a region of extreme social inequalities, including highly oppressive caste and gender relations' (Drèze & Sharma 1998: 9).

The publication 'Economic Development in Palanpur Over Five Decades', edited by Peter Lanjouw and Nicholas Stern (1998), is based on a series of five detailed surveys conducted by different economists starting in 1957-8 and ending in 1993 (Stern 1998: v). The team for the 1983-4 survey consisted of S.S. Tyagi Jr., Jean Drèze and Naresh Sharma who stayed in the village for fifteen months and collected their data using participant observation, informal discussions, questionnaires, interviews, government statistics and constant cross-checkings (Stern 1998: viii-ix). Drèze and Sharma returned to Palanpur for a few weeks in 1993 to carry out the fifth survey of the village. The most recent visit whose findings were included in the book was made by Drèze and Lanjouw in 1997.

There were three main castes in Palanpur, who were

> 'local representatives of three important sections of the rural society of Uttar Pradesh: the martial castes, which have played an influential role ... based on their high ritual status and strong temporal power at the local level, the cultivating castes, which often occupy a central position in the village economy, and also representing a growing political force and the 'scheduled castes', accounting for nearly a quarter of Uttar Pradesh's rural population' (Drèze & Sharma 1998: 31-32).

Thakurs, members of the martial caste, were at the 'top' of Palanpur's caste hierarchy. Muraos were the local representatives of the cultivating castes (Drèze & Sharma 1998: 29). While the Thakurs were politically still the most powerful caste in the village, they were 'no longer the unquestioned leaders of the village. Muraos, whose rising prosperity 'inspire[d] much respect in the village, ha[d] started challenging their supremacy' (Drèze & Sharma 1998: 33-34). The Jatabs, a 'Scheduled Caste', were the most marginalised citizens of Palanpur. Most of them were illiterate and extremely poor. They worked as casual wage labourers and cultivated small plots of land (Drèze & Sharma 1998: 31). The state had not helped them much. Drèze, Lanjouw and Sharma were disillusioned with regard to public services in Palanpur as the following summary shows:

> 'In Palanpur, as in most other Indian villages, people now have easier access to a whole range of public services and programmes' (Drèze, Lanjouw & Sharma 1998 (1): 181) ..., but 'the availability of public services and amenities in Palanpur is, for practical purposes, only marginally better now than it was at the beginning of the survey period. On Paper, Palanpur has everything: an 'Integrated Rural Development programme', a public employment programme, free schooling, free basic health care, immunization services, maternal health services, adult education, integrated care for pre-school children, family planning services, widows' pensions, old-age pensions, a fair price shop, agricultural extension, a farmer's cooperative, electricity, subsidized credit, collective water supply, land consolidation, etc. In practice, however, positive government intervention in Palanpur amounts to very little. Among these 18 types of programmes, we have noted a modicum of effectiveness for the last three, and at least some

benefits (if not the intended ones) for the first two. The remaining 13 are, for practical purposes, non-functional' (Drèze, Lanjouw & Sharma 1998 (1): 207).

The performance of selected public institutions in Palanpur warrants a closer look for the evaluation of the reasons for improvement and failures. The performance of the public primary school in Palanpur improved significantly over the survey period. In 1983-4 the school was run by the son of a former village Headmen, who 'more often than not, did not even take the trouble of coming to school at all', as his post was permanent and his salary, which was quite high by local standards, was not related to his performance (Drèze, Lanjouw & Sharma 1998 (1): 182). Villagers did not attempt to exert any collective pressure on him, even though there was a general understanding that education could be an important cause for upward economic mobility (Drèze, Lanjouw & Sharma 1998 (1): 187). The situation had improved slightly in 1993, because village teachers were not posted in their home villages anymore. Yet, 'the general view among Palanpur residents was that the village school … was still barely worth attending' (Drèze, Lanjouw & Sharma 1998 (1): 183). When Lanjouw and Drèze revisited the village in 1997, the situation had improved considerably. A total of fifty-five children were present when they visited the public school and it had three teachers. There was also a recently set up private school with one hundred and twenty pupils and although teaching standards were low, the researchers concluded that schooling had become the norm for children in Palanpur (Drèze, Lanjouw & Sharma 1998 (1): 232-3).

Even though there were public health care services available in nearby villages, they were rarely used by villagers, because they doubted the quality of the services, 'resent[ed] the brusque behaviour of the health staff, and expect[ed] to be asked to pay for services that [were] supposed to be free.' At least the District hospital in Moradabad seemed to deliver helpful services for those who had enough influence to be able to insist on getting the service according to the rules. But few villagers, if any, were in such a situation. Immunisation teams sometimes visited the village, but they did not deliver services, they only visited the Headman's house, filled some forms and left again. 'A similar lack of seriousness characterize[d] family planning and maternal health services, which [were] also … non-functional.' Villagers turned to one of three private practitioners (without any formal training) when they were ill and were usually treated with antibiotics. As medicine was expensive, some people took chances with folk medicine or simply hoped that the illness would go away again (Drèze, Lanjouw & Sharma 1998 (1): 190-1).

There was a government-run fair price shop in Palanpur in 1983-4 where citizens could buy kerosene and sugar at subsidized prices[17]. The manager, a Thakur with good connections to the Headman, opened the shop only sporadically and 'made no secret of the fact that he charged unofficial 'commissions' on all transactions.' He also sold items on the market for his own profit. In 1993, the shop had closed down and nobody seemed to miss it very much (Drèze, Lanjouw & Sharma 1998 (1): 193-4).

Only two cases of land redistribution had taken place in Palanpur during the survey period. In 1976, six households had received one acre of land each. The land was of extremely bad quality, barely cultivable. A close relative of the village Headman told the researchers that each beneficiary had to bribe the head of the local administrative unit and two officials beneath him. This was probably why the poorest households in the village did not get any land (Drèze, Lanjouw & Sharma 1998 (1): 191). Some more land had been distributed in 1997 when Lanjouw and Drèze returned to the village. All those who were landless and willing to undergo sterilization had been eligible. However, there were also a few wealthier families without land. Finally, 'those who had good relations with the village headman, a better ability to bribe the relevant officials, or other means of getting ahead of other eligible households', were the ones who were allotted land (Drèze, Lanjouw & Sharma 1998 (1): 232). The authors were of the opinion that moderate land redistribution would not meet with much resistance in Palanpur, if the government decided to pursue it seriously, which was not the case (Drèze, Lanjouw & Sharma 1998 (1): 192-3).

Since several households owned as many as eight plots of land, massive land consolidation took place in 1985-6. This operation was a modest success, even though some small farmers complained that they had lost land in the process while influential farmers had succeeded in obtaining improved holdings (Drèze, Lanjouw & Sharma 1998 (1): 204-6).

The Jawahar Rozgar Yojana (JRY) scheme, a Public Employment Programme was meant to boost the rural economy by giving jobs to unskilled workers and creating 'durable community assets'. The Panchayat (Village Council) was supposed to decide what should be build. Yet, in Palanpur and surrounding villages, Panchayats were not consulted and money from the scheme was used to plant trees (which quickly withered away due to a lack of proper care), and, more successfully, to pave village lanes. However, less than five percent of expenses went to unskilled labourers, Headmen preferred to employ skilled workers (Drèze, Lanjouw & Sharma 1998 (1): 195-6).

---

[17] Why these itmes were supposed to be more fundamental commodities than, for instance, rice or lentils, is difficult to understand.

There was also a credit cooperative in Palanpur, which most farmers belonged to. Even so, it was not managed by them, but by urban-based functionaries who used it to collect bribes from borrowers. Loans, which had been meant to be repaid within twelve months were 'rolled over' at the end of the year for a bribe of ten percent of the outstanding sum. There were also other corrupt practices such as taking up loans under the name of uninformed villagers. For those who could repay within a year and had enough clout to avoid having to pay large sums as bribes, the conditions were preferable. According to the interview partners, bribes were more frequently demanded from the poor than from the rich (Drèze, Lanjouw & Sharma 1998 (2): 525). Some farmers even had to sell part of their land to repay their debts, because of the excessive bribes they had to pay. As a result, they did not draw credit from the cooperative subsequently (Drèze, Lanjouw & Sharma 1998 (1): 198-9). This was a serious detriment, as the poor were often urgently in need of short-term loans, for example to feed their family when they had not found work for several days (Drèze, Lanjouw & Sharma (2) 1998: 506-7) or to buy seeds. They then had to turn to private moneylenders to whom they had to pay as much as 50 percent interest (Drèze, Lanjouw & Sharma (2) 1998: 506-7). In 1990, the government cancelled outstanding debts of the credit cooperative, but this was prinicpally to the benefit of privileged farmers who held a large part of institutional credit. Borrowers of the Integrated Rural Development Programme, targeted to poor households, were excluded from cancellations (Drèze, Lanjouw & Sharma 1998 (1): 198-9).

The Integrated Rural Development Programme (IRPD) was at the end of the 1980s the most important 'poverty alleviation programme' of the national government. It was a subsidised credit programme meant for households below the poverty line to buy productive assets like bullock carts or dairy livestock. The package of assistance, meant to go along with the loans, had never been seriously pursued. Since family income was hard to estimate, the Village Development Officer could virtually recommend anyone for the programme. In 1985, he collected a bribe of 200 Rupees from each household recommended (Drèze, Lanjouw & Sharma 1998 (1): 200-1). This bribe created a barrier for destitute households, whose poverty prevented them from participation in the scheme. Instead, sixty-seven percent of the selected households were in fact not eligible to participate, because they were too well off. So in terms of its own objectives, the programme was a failure (Drèze, Lanjouw & Sharma 1998 (1): 203-4).

The village of Palanpur was electrified twice, but each time the connecting wires were stolen, so that Palanpur continued to be without electricity in 1997 (Drèze, Lanjouw & Sharma 1998 (1): 197).

The most successful government scheme had been the installation of two public hand pumps, close to the quarters of the scheduled castes, which were extensively used (Drèze, Lanjouw & Sharma 1998 (1): 206-7).

The researchers summarised that nothing tangible had been achieved for the disadvantaged castes and classes in Palanpur. On the whole, the state of the public services was disastrous, especially for the most marginalised citizens. All programmes which especially targeted them or aimed at redistribution, failed, 'with the possible exception of water supply' (Drèze, Lanjouw & Sharma 1998 (1): 207). However, at least the performance of the public school had improved. Health care, though, seemed to be available only to those who could pay or had some influence. In order to buy from the ration shop - when it was open - customers had to pay 'commissions'. Land redistribution had hardly taken place, and when it had, beneficiaries had to bribe the government officers. Marginalised citizens did not profit from cooperative credit nor from IRPD-subsidised credits, because they could not afford the bribes to be paid.

Overall, though without the help of the state, most citizens of Palanpur had over the survey period been quite successful in 'averting the threat of impoverishment posed by rapid population growth on a small area of land'. This has been achieved through a combination of agricultural growth and expansion of non-agricultural employment. In both cases, private initiative and market forces had been the prime movers. Public institutions hardly helped. In fact, the government had not regulated the market, either. Even though there were 'plenty of official rules purporting to regulate labour transactions, tenancy agreements, credit contracts, marketing arrangements, and even food trade', none of these had been applied. Instead, an effectively unregulated market existed for almost everything (Drèze, Lanjouw & Sharma 1998 (1): 226).

The authors witnessed that the situation in the villages surrounding Palanpur was similar or worse. Widespread failure of development programmes was, as they argued, an important cause for 'the persistence of endemic deprivation in this region' (Drèze, Lanjouw & Sharma 1998 (1): 207-8). But as the next example will show, not all citizens in Uttar Pradesh responded to state inertia with passivity or resignation. The next two case studies in this chapter will present settings where, in the first case, an individual and in the second one, a movement tried to defend themselves against exploitation.

III.1.1.b. A Villager's Access to Development

In 1984-5 and again in 1989, the anthropologist Akhil Gupta did research in a small village in North India, which he calls 'Alipur'. In this village, several houses had been constructed under two government programmes, the Indira Awaas Yojana – the Indira Housing Programme meant for landless Harijans (Untouchables)[18] – and the Nibral Varg Awaas Yojana – the Weaker Sections Housing Programme intended for those who had less than one acre of land, no brick house and a low income.

Gupta talked to one of the beneficiaries of the programme, Sripal, a low caste (Gupta 1995: 381), illiterate (Gupta 1995: 382) young man, who related his story as follows. Sher Singh, the village Headman, had selected Sripal as a beneficiary for the scheme. The Village Development Worker[19] accompanied him into town to get his photograph taken and open an account in the bank, where he had to pay 200 Rupees for the paperwork. Sripal also paid for the transport of the building material and was asked to pay an additional 500 Rupees to get the bricks. Since he did not have the money, he asked the official to take material worth 1,000 Rupees from the quantity allotted to him instead. He had learned from talking to 'people who can read and write', that he was supposed to get material worth 7,000[20] Rupees, so after the deduction, he only got material worth 6,000 Rupees (Gupta 1995: 381). In addition, Sripal also had to settle the bill for the transport of the bricks (which, as he complained to Gupta, were improperly baked yellow bricks – Gupta 1995: 381). Since Sripal was an expert mason, he built his new house himself, but never received the 300 Rupees allotted for labour costs in the programme. Nor did he receive material for a door or windows. Furthermore, no one ever came to inspect whether the scheme had been executed properly. Sripal knew that inspectors just stayed in their offices, because, as he explained, 'they are the ones who have pen and paper' and thus the power to create the official record. All the same, Sripal did not give in, but lodged complaints at the Block Office and at the bank where he had borrowed money for the house. When the Headman found out about Sripal's complaint, he 'threatened to beat him up so badly that he would never enter the village again'. Frightened, Sripal fled to his in-laws. Since his complaints remained unanswered, he asked a lawyer to write a letter to the District Ma-

---

[18] The term 'Harijan' means Children of God. Mahatma Gandhi gave this name to the Untouchables. Lately, the term has come to be regarded as patronising. Increasingly often, the word Dalit, which has a more radical political connotation, is used today (Mendelsohn & Vicziany 1998: 2-5). Since all of my literature uses the term Harijan, I also to do so, in order not to create confusion for the readers. However, I do want to distance myself from any patronising connotation.

[19] The Village Development Worker is responsible for implementing development schemes in a small Circle of villages and, like other officials, gets a transfer to another posting every three years (Gupt 1995: 395).

[20] However, Gupta later found out that Rs. 8,000 were actually supposed to be allocated to each beneficiary (Gupta 1995: 395).

gistrate, the highest administrative authority in the area. This time, police came to the village to investigate the case. The Headman made peace with Sripal. Moreover, he employed him to construct a house. On the other hand, the Village Development Worker was not impressed. He asked Sripal to pay another 3000 Rupees and threatened to have him imprisoned by the jail warden – who was his relative – if he insisted on 'bilking'.

'Sitting in front of the empty space that was to be the door to his house, Sripal told [Gupta] that he was resigned to go to jail. 'What difference does it make?' he asked. 'Living like this is as good as being dead." (Gupta 1995: 382).

Like Sripal, other citizens are upset about exploitation by local officials and determined to make 'the state' work. The next case study will look at a collective and coordinated struggle to fight corruption and hold leaders accountable in Rajasthan.

III.1.1.c. A Social Movement in Rajasthan

The third case study is from an impoverished village, Devdungri, in the desert state of Rajasthan, where a people's movement for the right to information was started, led by activists of the Mazdoor Kisan Shakti Sangathan (MKSS). My information is based on a paper published by the 'Commonwealth Human Rights Initiative' in 1999 and authored by Harsh Mander and Abha Joshi, who visited the village in 1996. Harsh Mander used to be a high-ranking officer in the elite Indian Administrative Service (IAS) and became famous when he publicly resigned from his post, stating his disgust with the civil service's inertia during the anti-Muslim riots in Gujarat. His report is neither based on an ethnographic enquiry, nor written by an impartial observer, but by a social activist who widely campaigns for anti-corruption measures (Phukan). Still, it is very valuable for my paper. Harsh Mander looks back upon long experiences of the inner workings of the state machinery, which he probably understands at least as well as any social scientist, and has won respect for his moral uprightness in India. While, as Corbridge et al. (2005: 223) remark, it is certainly true, 'that there is a pressing need for independent assessments of the activities of the MKSS and the effectiveness of its Jan Sunvais', as they also acknowledge, 'it is hard to escape the conclusion, even so, that the MKSS has enjoyed considerable success in Rajasthan'. I use the paper because of the significance of the MKSS movement for my investigation, because no ethnographic enquiry into a comparable social movement is available, and because the report presents a detailed analysis of the local workings of the movement.

Devdungri lied in an area which was drought-prone and environmentally degraded. Land holdings were so small that people often went hungry even when there was a good monsoon. Famine relief projects did not help much, because corruption was rampant. Less than two percent of the women and about twenty-six percent of the men were literate. Out-migration was high and the average debt burden was more than 3,200 Rupees per household, an enormous sum for the poor (Joshi & Mander 1999: 7).

In 1987, three founding members of the MKSS (which was formally registered in 1990) set themselves up in this village. Aruna Roy was a retiree from the Indian Administrative Service, Shankar Singh and his family came from a nearby village and Nikhil Dey was a young student who had abandoned his studies in the USA. They had resolved not to accept outside funding and live with no more amenities than the locals had. Thus, they did neither have electricity nor water nor a car and their diet was extremely poor. In the following years, they supported numerous non-violent local struggles and earned a good reputation among the locals (Joshi & Mander 1999: 6-8).

In 1994, the MKSS initiated the first 'Jan Sunvai', a people's audit, in which all documents related to public works were to be presented to and discussed by the people in order to uncover possible irregularities. The activists looked at muster rolls, which showed the attendance of workers and wages paid, as well as bills and vouchers for the purchase and transport of material. These documents were read out to the people (Joshi & Mander 1999: 9) by the facilitators who paraphrased the formal language of the documents to 'demystify' them for the assembly (Joshi & Mander 1999: 23). A long list of irregularities was uncovered. The villagers

> 'learnt that a large number of persons, some long dead or migrated or non-existent, were listed as workers and shown to be paid wages which were siphoned away, that as many bags of cement were said to have been used in the 'repair' of a primary school building as would be adequate for a new building, and innumerable other such stunning facts of the duplicity and fraud of the local officials and elected representatives' (Joshi & Mander 1999: 9).

Even before the Jan Sunvai, the illiterate villagers had been aware of the misappropriation of public funds, but in the absence of evidence and support, they had no means of interfering with it. 'The public hearings dramatically changed this, and ordinary people spoke out fearlessly and gave convincing evidence against corruption' (Joshi & Mander 1999: 9), in the immediate presence of Village Council members and government officials from the District, Block and village level, who had also been invited to defend themselves.

While officials in the area generally attended the Jan Sunvais, they often tried to obstruct them during the preparatory phase. For one public meeting to be held in 1998, the Collector (a higher-ranking bureaucrat) ordered that copies of muster rolls, bills and vouchers should be given to the activists, but the Village Development officers refused to obey him. Instead, they initiated a strike against this order which spread to the entire state of Rajasthan (Joshi & Mander 1999: 9-10). The MKSS still went ahead with its meeting and was able to gather evidence of corruption even without the requested documents. This evidence was presented to the Collector, who visited the gathered villagers of Bagmal for an official investigation into the accusations.

'However, 24 Sarpanches or elected village heads of surrounding villages who had nothing to do with the enquiry in progress, arrived at the spot and raised an uproar. A woman Sarpanch tore the shirt of a villager giving evidence. The official remained silent, but shifted his enquiry indoors. Threats and assaults on the villagers and activists continued subsequently' (Joshi & Mander 1999: 10).

However, after the official enquiry, the administration of the four Districts, in which the MKSS had initiated Jan Sunvais and gathered evidence of corruption, still refused to register criminal cases or attempt to recover stolen money (Joshi & Mander 1999: 10).

From the very beginning, Jan Sunvais were getting considerable publicity and activists were even invited to the famous Lal Bahadur Shastri National Academy of Administration in Mussoorie in 1995. The Chief Minister of Rajasthan, meanwhile, promised in the state legislature that his government would be the first in the country to grant citizens the right to photocopies of all documents related to local development works. However, even a year later, nothing had happened. Harsh Mander hypothesised,

'This lapse of faith was presumably under pressure both from elected representatives and officials connected with such works, who regard as their birthright the illegal siphoning off of major portions of such expenditure' (Joshi & Mander 1999: 11).

In the midst of an election campaign 'shrill in its hypocrisy regarding corruption', the MKSS and more than 500 citizens from diverse political and social backgrounds – 'from rich shopkeepers and professionals to daily wage labourers' (Joshi & Mander 1999: 12) – decided to launch a dharna[21] in the town of Beawar in 1996. They were supported by surrounding villages:

'Donations in cash and kind poured in daily from ordinary local people, including vegetables and milk from small vendors, sacks of

---

[21] A dharna is a fast conducted at the door of an offender as a means of obtaining compliance with a demand for justice.

wheat from farmers in surrounding villages, tents, voluntary services of cooking, serving cold water, photography and so on, and cash donations from even the poorest. ... Active support cut across all class and political barriers' (Joshi & Mander 1999: 12).

This is when Abha Joshi and Harsh Mander visited the scene and witnessed among ordinary people a

> 'surprisingly high awareness of the issues involved. 'Why cannot the government give us information regarding expenditures made in our name?' passionately demanded a waiter in a tea-stall. 'It is a fight for justice for the poor' affirmed the owner of a pavement shop selling rubber footwear. Everyone we spoke to was unanimous that there was no other agitation since Independence to which women and men from all backgrounds extended such unstinted support and in which they saw so much hope' (Joshi & Mander 1999: 12).

After the election, the dharna spread to the state capital of Jaipur. More than 70 people's organisations, well-known citizens as well as the mainstream press expressed their sympathy to the cause. The government gave in and established a committee to work out the details of the new order (Joshi & Mander 1999: 13). However, another year passed with no notable changes to the situation, so a second dharna was initiated in the capital. After 52 days,

> 'the Deputy Chief Minister made an astonishing announcement, that six months earlier, the state government had already notified the right to receive photo-copies of documents related to Panchayat or village local government institutions. Why such an order, ironically related to transparency, had been kept a secret, even during the 52-day dharna, remained a mystery. Nevertheless, the order of the state government was welcomed as a major milestone, because for the first time, it recognised the legal entitlement of ordinary citizens to obtain copies of government held documents' (Joshi & Mander 1999: 14).

However, as I have already cautioned in the discussion of legalistic approaches to the study of corruption (compare chapter I.4.3), passing laws is not sufficient, they must still be implemented, another struggle that lay ahead of the people. Therefore, 'the MKSS and other organisations set about organising people to use this important entitlement'. As expected, they continued 'to face in a majority of cases an obstinate bureaucracy and recalcitrant local government representatives who still refused to supply copies of documents.' They responded by complaining to superiors and mobilising people 'to mount peaceful democratic agitational pressure on the authorities' (Joshi & Mander 1999: 14).

In Harmara, for example, the village Headman refused to deliver copies of documents related to public works in his area. MKSS workers kept visiting him at his office and later also at his home, where they were 'manhandled and pushed out', after which both the Headman and the MKSS filed complaints at the police station. The 'Rajasthan State Campaign Committee on Right to Information' and the state 'People's Union for Civil Liberties' organised a dharna, but to no avail. Another dharna was launched at the Sub-Divisional headquarters of Kishengarh. Subsequently, the Headman turned over documents, but only three out of the twenty requested. The Block Office issued copies of thirteen muster rolls, but not bills or vouchers. Although the Collector ordered a special audit and seizure of the documents, this was not implemented. In Kukurheda, in contrast, following several requests, complaints to superior authorities and a two-week dharna, the Headman surrendered all documents (Joshi & Mander 1999: 15).

Another difficulty was to convince superior officials (who might be complicit) to initiate legal action against corrupt colleagues or politicians. In Kukurheda, the woman Sarpanch 'publicly accepted her guilt in a charge of corruption in public works to the tune of 100,000 Rupees, and during the Jan Sunwai itself returned the first instalment of 50,000 Rupees. The amount was deposited in the Panchayat fund.' This was perceived to be an important victory. Two days later, the Block Development Officer (BDO) looked into the case and also established evidence of corruption. But instead of registering a criminal charge against the woman, he and the other Headmen of the Block persuaded her to resign. She stepped down, but only after having taken the 50,000 Rupees back out of the Panchayat fund, for which she was not charged subsequently.

In Ajmer District, on the other hand, two Sarpanches who had returned misappropriated money during a people's audit, also had to go to jail, because the Collector filed a case against them. (Joshi & Mander 1999: 24).

III.1.2.1. Citizens & Corruption: Findings

In the following chapter, I will summarise the most important findings generated from the analysis of the case studies presented above and also draw on further literature to underline my points. I will start by looking at how marginalised citizens encounter corruption and emphasise that they are the ones who suffer worst at the hands of exploitative officials, both because they are unable to substitute defunct public services by costly private facilities and because bribes are most often demanded from those who are poorest and not from the wealthy, who are more influential. This will lead to the next two chapters, in which I will look at the reasons for the failure of public services. My first hypothesis is that the reasons for malfunctioning public services are to be sought in politics and divergent elite interests. Another factor contributing to citizen's exploitation is their lack of proper information about entitlements and procedures, a point made in the following chapter. The next chapters look at how citizens handle malfunctioning public services and how officials and politicians react to their behaviour. In the final chapter, I will summarise, what attitude towards the state might arise among marginalised citizens from their encounters with corrupt politicians and bureaucrats.

III.1.2.a. Public Services for Whom?

As explored in section III of the paper, after Independence the Indian state was assigned numerous developmental and welfare responsibilities.

> 'In India today, the state has spread its tentacles to virtually every aspect of public life. The person on the street is condemned to grapple hopelessly with corruption in almost every aspect of daily work and living' (Joshi and Mander 1999: 2).

Out of the many public schemes and services in Palanpur, however, most worked exclusively to the benefit of the upper classes. Marginalised citizens were most negatively affected by the failure of redistributive measures as well as the malfunctioning of public services, which could have significantly improved their situation. Credit, health care or land redistribution, for example, were not available to them without bribes. Due to a lack of financial resources, poor citizens could neither pay officials to do what they were supposed to do nor turn to private providers of the services needed. Thus, as Dougherty had warned, (compare chapter I.4.2) corruption in this situation cannot be adequately described as a 'weapon of the weak', or at least not of the weakest.

Like villagers in Palanpur, other citizens in India are also almost completely marginalised from state services in spite of the existence of democracy and a free media in India, which are supposed to give voice to subalterns (compare chapter I.2.2). In her article on the infamous tribal Kalahandi District of Orissa, Jayal re-examined the theory that democracy and a free press could prevent famines. She argued that it did not hold true. Instead, politicians denied the existence of famines even though they actually occured. In complicity with rich farmers, moneylenders and contractors, state officials did not protect citizens from hunger, but even extracted money from them:

> 'Neither the massive funding for emergency feeding and gratuitous relief, nor the somewhat lower levels of development funds, have however reduced the vulnerability of the poor to hunger, or rendered them

capable of independent means of survival. Resources have flowed into Kalahandi, but have generally come in late, misutilized, misadministered, and possibly even misappropriated on their way to those for whom they were intended' (Jayal 2001 (2): 201).

The performance of the local state was equally poor, as the Mishra Commission, which investigated the first widely-publicised cases of death due to hunger, had documented.

'The local state – as the Mishra Commission showed – ha[d] been indifferent and apathetic, often making common cause with local elites, rich farmers, moneylenders and contractors. ... Evidence abound[ed] of bank officials who routinely appropriate[d] a large portion of the loans they grant[ed]; of profiteering by middlemen in the administration of employment programmes; of the intimidation of the poor by family planning officials; of the bribery and corruption rampant even in the Welfare Extension Office; and of the illegal 'selling' and transfers of vast amounts of tribal land' (Jayal 2001 (2): 203).

Even after the publication of the study, nothing changed. In summary it can be said that state officials in Kalahandi exploited the starving poor without even providing them with education or health care facilities. Similar disastrous cases of the failure of the state and its deadly consequences have been documented, for instance, by Paul Brass in his ethnography 'Theft of an Idol. Text and Context in the Representation of Collective Violence' (1998), in which he discussed the involvement of the police in 'state-sponsored violence'[22]. A third example is the study 'Power, Poverty and Posion. Disaster and Response in an Indian City' by James Manor (1993), in which state officials' failure to control the sale of poisonous illicit alcohol is shown to have killed several slum inhabitants. In both studies, the authors showed that political forces had been in complicity with the criminals.

Less spectacular, 'everyday failures of the state' as in Palanpur, are commonplace and equally disastrous in their consequences for the poor, who cannot easily afford substitutes for public services. Corbridge and Harris (2000: 202) point out that

---

[22] The main focus of his study was on the interpretation of local riots offered by the media and politicians. In his analysis, however, he also showed that local leaders competed for control of the police forces. While it might be an exaggeration to speak of 'lawlessness' in rural India, what 'we have [is] a network of power relations among police, criminals and politicians in which the use of violence is, if not routine, at least not something unexpected or exceptional' (Brass 1998: 275 – compare chapter III.3.2.a for rural power relations and the use of violence).

'[a]s a trip to any Block Office in Bihar will confirm, poorer men and women - and especially women - will be kept waiting for hours or even days to gain access to a government officer responsible for the allocation of pensions or some other benefit'.

Van Kampen (2000) witnessed similar problems during his field research on development and participation in two squatter settlements in Pune:

'Some women alleged that they faced difficulties in entering an office and that sometimes they were not allowed to go inside. We tested this and found that they were indeed treated differently from assertive and well-educated (middle-class) people. On some occasions they were 'refused' access, for instance, by a peon who told them that they had come to the wrong place or at the wrong time (he may have tried to get a bribe) ...' (van Kampen 2000: 323).

III.1.2.b. Who has to Bribe?

Marginalised citizens are excluded from government services because they often lack effective means of defending themselves against unjust behaviour or exploitation. In Palanpur, they did not profit from land redistribution, cooperative credit or IRPD-subsidised credits, although these were especially for them. In each case, bribes, which the poor could not afford, had to be paid to officials in order to benefit. Poorer clients were also prime victims of mounting extortion, because,

'[p]overty, illiteracy and low social status all reduce the *bargaining power* of a borrower, and enhance his or her vulnerability to fraudulent procedures' (Drèze, Lanjouw & Stern 1998 (2): 525, my italics).

Because of this, especially the poor had to bribe officials if they wanted to benefit from government schemes. While those who had enough resources to pay the bribes obviously thought it worthwhile to spend their money for the allocation of land or credit, the most marginalised citizens could not partake in the benefits of government programmes. However, Marguerite Robinson (1988: 11) added a historical perspective to the discussion of corruption which other case studies lacked. She argued, that it was already a significant change that marginalised citizens were at all able to bribe officials directly once they had raised the money necessary to do so (compare chapter III.3.3.g for further elaboration).

III.1.2.c. Political Reasons

As the example of the intricate, yet successful land consolidation in Palanpur showed, the reasons for the malfunctioning of public services were not mainly administrative, but essentially political. Schemes such as land consolidation which had the backing of influential groups or players were successful – 'even when their administrative requirements ha[d] been quite exacting' (Drèze, Lanjouw & Stern 1998 (1): 210).

Many important posts in Palanpur were held by upper class villagers with good relations to the Headman – for example the teacher of the public school or the manager of the ration shop mentioned earlier. That is why state institutions hardly worked for the poor:

> 'The agenda of state policy [was] dominated by the demands of privileged classes, the village Panchayat [was] virtually non-functional, and the successive Headmen ha[d] used their position to further their own interest more than those of the community. The reach of informal collective action ha[d] also been very limited, partly due to the fragmented nature of the village society' (Drèze, Lanjouw & Sharma 1998 (1): 228).

So far, marginalised citizens in Palanpur had not tried to challenge the domination – and exploitation – by local 'uppers' through collective action. Drèze, Lanjouw and Stern concluded that for Palanpur,

> '[t]here [was] little prospect of major improvement in the orientation and achievements of government intervention without a significant change in the balance of political power, both at the state and at the local level. Democratic institutions provide a potential basis for such a change, but their actual impact has remained quite limited so far' (Drèze, Lanjouw & Stern 1998 (1): 211).

Other citizens, however, have tried to make use of democratic institutions to check elite behaviour as the other two case studies presented above have shown. The findings drawn from analysing them will be presented below.

III.1.2.d. Information & Empowerment

While it is true that the reasons for the malfunctioning of public services are essentially political, 'opaque rules and procedures' play an important part in confusing and 'scaring away' marginalised citizens from public services.

> 'Most government offices typically present a picture of a client public bewildered and harassed by opaque rules and procedures and inordinate delays, constantly vulnerable to exploitation by employees and touts' (Joshi & Mander 1999: 2).

Many of the poor and illiterate do not know how the formalised system works and are therefore open to middlemen's, bureaucrats' and politicians' attempts to exploit them. When van Kampen's (2000: 323) informants in the squatter settlement in Pune tried to apply for ration cards[23], 'officials did not provide the required information or failed to do so in a comprehensible manner.' His study on 'Anti-poverty Policy and Popular Participation in two Squatter Settlements' concluded that

> 'The procedures are troublesome for the poor. Several inhabitants of Rangit Vasahat tried to follow this formal path and failed, which is not surprising. In general, the application procedures of formal anti-poverty initiatives, particularly those of the state, are too complicated and too bureaucratic. They are even more complicated if not impossible for illiterate women ... Unfortunately, they are the ones who need the cards most' (van Kampen 2000: 323).

In my research report about the nomadic Van Gujjar in Uttaranchal, I concluded that rights were only for those who knew how to handle the procedures. Illiterates like the Van Gujjar, tribals in Kalahandi, or marginalised citizens in Palanpur or Pune, however, were at the mercy of those more knowledgeable or powerful, as, for instance, state or police officers. As Niraja Gopal Jayal reported for famine struck Kalahandi:

> 'The landless tribal poor [were] implicitly governed as subjects rather than citizens. Lacking effective citizenship, they also lack[ed] rights. Lacking information – and the means or opportunity to acquire it – they lack[ed] also the werewithal to access democratic institutions and processes through which to articulate their demands' (Jayal 2001: 202).

That is why marginalised citizens all over India emphasise the importance of education for their children (compare chapter II.4.1). However, tribal or low caste illiterates are not necessarily helpless as the example of Sripal powerfully demonstrated. He used his connection to educated people 'who [could] read and write' to find out about government schemes. He also knew about the multiple 'layers of the state', as Gupta (1995: 387) put it – and used this knowledge by appealing to the superiors of those officers and politicians who demanded illicit payments and threatened to use physical force against him. Sripal also knew about his rights and entitlements and decided to insist on getting what was due to him, even if he had to go to jail. However, to learn about complicated bureaucratic procedures, guidelines, laws and hierarchies one can appeal to, may involve high opportunity costs for those who are less educated or without good connections. The media and public discussions, however, can play an important part in the circulation of necessary information as will be discussed further in Chapter III.3.3.c.

---

[23] Citizens who posess a ration card, can buy at subsidised prices from the government-run 'fair price shops' (compare chapter III.1.1.a).

Looking at the social movement in Rajasthan, the success of the Jan Sunvais is striking when compared to the failure of the Village Assemblies (Gram Sabhas), which had long been 'specifically empowered under the law, to conduct a social audit into all rural development programmes'. Gram Sabhas in the region, however, were often defunct and members were 'unaware or cynical about their rights' (Joshi & Mander 1999: 21). It seems obvious that the activists of the MKSS, educated facilitators from the outside, were vital for the success of the Jan Sunvais its force. They had informed the villagers

> 'about their rights, encourage[d] the victims of injustice and disadvantaged groups to speak out ... [and] ensure[d] that information [was] placed before the participants in a comprehensible manner, that decisions taken [were] legally recorded, and follow-up ensured' (Joshi & Mander 1999: 21).

The role of the facilitators was of central importance, because most villagers were illiterate and did not know enough about formal procedures (Joshi & Mander 1999: 23). 'As agents of hitherto exclusive information', facilitators may be tempted by a sense of power and a new dependency of the marginalised arise. Recognising this danger, Joshi and Mander (1999: 23) suggested that facilitators should be trained to resist 'exercising personal power'. Although new dependencies might be difficult to avoid in mobilising the poor, in the long run, only measures enabling citizens to get information independently, can lead to sustainable empowerment.

> 'sources of corruption are inherent within the character of the state machine. These include a determined denial of transparency, accessibility and accountability, cumbersome and confusing procedures, proliferation of mindless controls, and poor commitment at all levels to real results of public welfare. In this section, we will argue that information is power, and that the executive at all levels attempts to withhold information to increase its scope for control, patronage, and the arbitrary, corrupt and unaccountable exercise of power. Therefore, *demystification of rules and procedures, complete transparency and pro-active dissemination of this relevant information amongst the public is potentially a very strong safeguard against corruption.* ... Information is the currency that every citizen requires to participate in the life and governance of society. The greater the access of the citizen to information, the greater would be the responsiveness of government to community needs. Alternatively, the greater the restrictions that are placed on access, the greater the feelings of `powerlessness' and 'alienation'. Without information, people cannot adequately exercise their rights and responsibilities as citizens or make informed choices' (Joshi and Mander 1999: 2-3, my italics).

III.1.2.e. How Citizens Handle Public Services

After bad experiences with government banks, poorer villagers in Palanpur tried to stay away from government programmes altogether. There was too much insecurity involved, as they had little chance of fighting illicit extortion (Drèze, Lanjouw & Stern 1998 (1): 210). They did not take collective action either, 'partly due to the fragmented nature of the village society', as the authors supposed (Drèze, Lanjouw & Sharma 1998 (1): 228). The situation in the villages surrounding Palanpur was similar or worse. Widespread failure development programmes was, as the authors argued, the main cause for 'the persistence of endemic deprivation in this region' (Drèze, Lanjouw & Sharma 1998 (1): 207-8).

But while 'it is true that a certain amount of government inertia, corruption, and inefficiency can be found everywhere in the country', there are wide disparities (Drèze, Lanjouw & Sharma 1998 (1): 208). The next two case studies introduced situations where an individual, in the first case and a movement, in the second one, attempted to challenge existing structures of domination and exploitation.

Gupta's ethnography (1995) showed how difficult it is even for a brave and persistent person like Sripal to avoid exploitation by the Headman and the Village Development Worker. Yet, it also showed that marginalised citizens are not without means of defence. Although Sripal was illiterate and from a low caste, he was determined to get what he was entitled to. He employed his knowledge to appeal to superiors and even employed a lawyer to draft a complaint to the District Magistrate. He exploited the fact that,

> 'in the implementation of development programs, for example, local officials often have to seek out beneficiaries in order to meet targets set by higher authorities. The beneficiaries of these programs can then employ the authority of the upper levels of the bureaucracy to exert some pressure on local officials' (Gupta 1995: 381).

In Devdungri, social activists joined forces with local villagers and initiated a social movement for the right to information in order to make the government more accountable to the citizens. They used public meetings, in which local government's records were inspected by concerned citizens in order to find out about misappropriation of funds. The movement gained widespread support from different sections of society.

This seems to suggest, that corruption is an issue concerning and upsetting diverse citizens and that they are potentially willing to take on together. It also shows that collective action can be so powerful that local leaders are force to retreat. However, it is necessary to inspect whether this does in fact ead to new power relations between the village elite and the marginalised.

III.1.2.f. Officials' and Politicians' Reactions

Sripal's first appeals to superiors at the Bank and the Block Office were not answered. However, there was a reaction to the letter the lawyer had written to the District Magistrate. Police was sent to the village to investigate, which signalled to the Headman that physical harm to the scheduled caste Sripal would not be tolerated by the authorities. Although the Village Development Worker persisted in his demands and tried to invoke Sripal's fear by threatening to imprison him, the Headman retreated and even employed Sripal for the construction of a house, an indication of Sripal's improved standing. Likewise, Robinson (1988: 11) asserted in her ethnographic study of political change in a village in Andhra Pradesh that the state sometimes helped lower castes directly, by-passing local elites (compare chapter III.3.2.a).

While the Jan Sunvai Movement gained widespread support from different citizens, the elite whose corrupt side earnings and power were threatened, was upset.

> 'It is important to note that the other side also mobilises ... in a variety of ways, through persuasion, appeals to class, caste and clan loyalties, threats and covert or overt violence (Joshi & Mander 1999: 22).

The range of reactions from the official side was extensive. While some politicians physically attacked villagers in a meeting, although the Collector, a high ranking administrative authority was present and conducted an official investigation (Joshi & Mander 1999: 10), other instances of overt violence have not been reported by Joshi and Mander, maybe because the movement, thanks to the MKSS activists, was getting good press coverage from the beginning and widespread support, including that of the state's Chief Minister (Joshi & Mander 1999: 11). The village Headman of Harmara, for instance, was obviously frightened, because he secretly paid the enormous sum of previously withheld 150,000 Rupees to workers since the process of the Jan Sunvais began in his village. While the village headwoman in Kukurheda got away although she had misappropriated 100.000 Rupees, in Ajmer District two village Headmen had to pay back misappropriated money and received prison sentences, because the Collector, a higher level bureaucrat, had filed a case against them.

As these examples show, the registering of criminal charges depended on the goodwill of supervising officials. Joshi and Mander suggest that 'recourse to some kind of organised peaceful protest seems inevitable, if state authorities remain recalcitrant' (Joshi & Mander 1999: 25). This is underlined by the fact that even after the state government had issued an order to give photocopies of public documents to citizens, many officials refused to obey.

As this shows, implementing reformes can be difficult, (compare chapter I.4.3) because ruling elites will not easily give up their power. However, the difficulties faced by the movement in spite of widespread public and media support is also an indicator of its potential success. It seems as if corrupt politicians and bureaucrats felt threatened by the process, while those who were not corrupt might have been encouraged to behave as was legally expected of them. As a bureaucrat remarked on another occasion (see chapter III.2.3.g): 'The people's right to know has become our right to 'no'' (Joshi & Mander 1999: 28).

Even politicians could not help but support the quest for more accountability, at least in election campaign speeches. The movement shows how much scope there is for joint action in a democracy with a free press such as India, in spite of all its other shortcomings (compare chapter I.2.2).

III.1.2.g. Attitudes Towards the State

Before the process of the Jan Sunvais began in Devdungri, Village Assemblies (Gram Sabhas) in the area were mostly defunct and members 'unaware or cynical about their rights', related Harsh and Mander (1999: 21). Van Kampen (2000: 323) reported from squatter settlements in Pune, that many marginalised citizens were demotivated from visiting public institutions, because of a lack of time, information and money and due to 'previous bad experience and hearsay'. Furthermore, the poor in Palanpur also avoided getting involved with government services, as they were prime victims of fraud and often ended up worse if they put their trust in public institutions, as the example of subsidised credit had proved: 'Beneficiaries' had to pay so much bribes to officials, that they were more indebted in the end and some had to sell land to clear their loans (Drèze, Lanjouw & Sharma 1998 (2): 523).

> 'Years of … dishonest accounting ha[d] transformed their tiny initial dues into back-breaking liabilities' (Drèze, Lanjouw & Sharma 1998 (2): 525).

As Bawa and Jain noted, many citizens had become accustomed to bribery.

> 'The existence of a colossal public cynicism towards it, people's acceptance of corruption in public life and the feeling that those indicted of political corruption invariably got scot-free and in the process amass more 'power, status and wealth' have led to a situation, where even the most determined efforts to fight the evil have failed' (Bawa & Jain 2003: 16).

However, Sripal's attitude was different. He did not stay away from the government's housing scheme, but took on the challenge. While he did pay money, for instance for the transport of bricks and paperwork at the bank, he tried to ensure he was getting what he was supposed to, by asking educated people about the details of the scheme. When the material for his door and window were not delivered, he complained to superior officials and went as far as employing a lawyer. He did not give in even after having been threatened with physical force. At this point, he was not willing to pay any more money. His awareness of his rights and his determination may be explained by looking at his surroundings. As Gupta witnessed, corruption was hotly debated in Sripal's village.

> 'While doing fieldwork in a small village in North India ... most of the stories the men told each other in the evening when the day's work was done and small groups had gathered at habitual places to shoot the breeze, had to do with corruption (bhrashtaachar) and 'the state'. ... Sometimes the discussion dealt with how someone had managed to outwit an official who wanted to collect a bribe; at other times with 'the going price' to get an electrical connection for a new tube well or to obtain a loan to get a buffalo; at still other times with which official had been transferred or who was likely to be appointed to a certain position and who replaced, with who had willingly helped his caste members or relatives without taking a bribe, and so on. Sections of the penal code were discussed in great detail, the legality of certain actions to circumvent normal procedure were hotly debated, the pronouncements of District officials discussed at great length' (Gupta 95: 375).

Citizens in 'Alipur' were thus quite aware of their rights. Legal rules and procedures were of great importance to their discussions. While it is certainly true, as Stern had (1998: 234) argued that 'the impact of legislative reforms is highly contingent on social conditions', the example of Alipur shows that rules can have a normative power even if they are not implemented properly (compare chapters I.4.3; III.2.3.9; III.3.3.c and IV). While familism, casteism and communalism sometimes played a part in helping clients to avoid having to bribe, this was by no means universal. In fact, as Parry related for a very different situation (getting a job in a public plant), his informants told him that helping kinsmen without charging money became increasingly rare, except for very close relatives (compare chapters I.4.1, III.3.3.e, IV).

Like Sripal, other villagers might be mistrustful of the state, but pragmatic in their approach to its officials and determined to fight for their share of the spoils. Because Sripal was aware of his rights, he was not willing to give them up easily. Rather, he resolved to force the state to act as it was supposed to for his individual benefit. He knew that he was a possible victim of fraud, yet he tried to resist, even if he had to go to jail. The risk he was prepared to take might indicate that he did not simply make a rational choice by opting for what gave him the best profit most easily, but might instead have been committed to the idea he was defending; the idea that the state – or rather its officials – should be forced to work according to the rules.

The same awareness was created in Devdungri through the establishment of the Jan Sunvais. Even if some Jan Sunvais were unsuccessful, due to constant pressures from local leaders as well as their superior allies, the awareness the process created was a merit in itself. People witnessed that local leaders relented under the pressure brought about by collective action, an experience, an idea, they will certainly not forget. As Khilnani said about the impact of the idea of democracy in India:

> 'Democracy ... as an idea, as a seductive and puzzling promise to bring history under the command of the will of a community of equals – a promise that, given the inevitable gap between intentions and consequences, can at best only hope for partial fulfilment – it has irreversibly entered the political imagination. A return to the old order of castes, or rule of empire, is inconceivable: the principle of authority in society has been transformed' (Khilnani 2004: 60).

The social movement for the right to information has made citizens aware of the power they have in a democracy like India and it has also become evident that there is a potential for uniting rather diverse social players on moral grounds. Unlike Sripal, citizens in Devdungri did not only fight for 'their share of the spoils', rather the aim of their fight was to fundamentally improve the rules and institutions of the state so that officials would become more accountable in the long run.

III.1.2.h. Citizens Making Sense of Corruption

In summary, the citizens we have looked at, were aware that the state was an institution that had significant and vital basic resources, such as land, education, health care, and much more, to distribute. However, these resources were often appropriated by the elite in various ways, which marginalised citizens generally despised of and judged to be illegitimate. In some cases, citizens became cynical about the 'ideas' of India, about the promises of development and democracy again and again made to them in election speeches. In other cases, however, marginalised citizens decided not to put up with the injustice being done to them and challenged the elite in various ways. They were demanding what the state had promised and were developing powerful and determined means of peaceful, and also violent, resistance. It might be true that, as I had speculated in the discussion of theoretical approaches (compare chapter I.4.3), the 'ideas of

India' have become such a powerful vision that citizens now expect them to become true. Seeing the failure, some citizens become frustrated, others become angry and decide to fight, in order to get access to state resources, and / or to make the state work according to the rules[24].

III.2. The Bureaucracy

In the following chapter, I will look at those who are accused of taking bribes from citizens. After giving a short introduction to the Indian bureaucracy, I will try to show under what logic – and pressures – officials operate by looking at three case studies. Thereafter I will summarise the propositions generated from looking at the former, as well as additional case studies that will be introduced where appropriate.

III.2.1. Introduction to the Indian Bureaucracy

Bureaucrats hold a considerable degree of power, because they are the ones who 'actually undertake the tasks of government', while the government only sets forth 'general policy statements' (Dye & Zeigler 2003: 314).

'The bureaucrats control information and technology, and they almost invariably outlast their political superiors in office. ... The power of bureaucracies grows with advances in technology, increases in information and growth and complexity of society' (Dye & Zeigler 2003: 286).

The Indian bureaucracy oversees 'the vast policy-implementation machinery of the state' and helps to 'formulate major policies' (Pavarala: 31). The first Indian Prime Minister, Nehru gave a large number of developmental responsibilities to the bureaucracy out of political considerations. He hoped

---

[24] However, one very important qualification, which seriously darkens the picture painted, remains to be mentioned. As I have said in chapter III.1.2.a the failure of the state to protect its citizens – or provide them with the means to live decently – regularly has deadly consequences, especially when there is a crisis such as a riot or a drought – which may actually occur quite regularly. Keeping this in mind, it is not too difficult to understand that there are also citizens and groups who respond to this systemic violence with physical violence of their own, especially in regions where land distribution is highly unequal. One group which must be named here are the Naxalites, Marx-inspired Communist groups fighting against the elite in a number of Eastern Indian states presently (van Riel 2006). 'The ideological thrust of the extreme left', in general, has been 'towards overthrowing the state rather than engaging with its developmental agenda' (Corbridge et al 2005: 117). Unfortunately, the Naxalites and other rebel groups cannot be introduced nor discussed further at this point, as I have opted for a different focus, on everyday corruption in situations of relative peace and stability. For indirect effects of class violence, however, compare chapter III.3.3.b and III.3.3.g.

to use them to carry out his developmental vision in spite of – and against 'the obstructions raised by his own party' (Khilnani 2004: 81).

> 'The result was a leap in its [the bureaucracy's] size and power: an expansionary movement that by the 1970s had become unstoppable, driven by a regime of proliferating licenses and regulations. The public bureaucracy duly installed itself as yet another parasitic claimant on the state's resources' (Khilnani 2004: 81).

Because 'the state assumed increasing prominence in the allocation of resources and the control of economic activities', the bureaucracy became an important centre of power in the Indian polity (Pavarala: 29). Hence, the opportunities for illicit extortion also increased. Bawa and Jain, writing about corruption in India, remarked that 'bureaucratic corruption in the Third World tends to differ from that of the industrialised countries in its scope and intensity', because of a variety of reasons. As mentioned in the discussion of economic approaches to the study of corruption (compare chapter I.4.2; III.2.3.d), in many of the financially weaker countries, the clash between the 'scarcity of public resources and almost unlimited demand by the community give rise to … corrupt and unethical practices'. Additionally, there is a scarcity of jobs and even jobs in the public sector are insufficiently salaried (Bawa & Jain 2003: 28). In India,

> 'administrative corruption … has also been encouraged by the pervasive spread of the soft-state syndrome, a rigid bureaucracy, exclusivist process of decision-making in an over-centralised government, abysmally low pay of civil servants and lack of stringent and effective internal control mechanisms' (Bawa & Jain 2003: 28).

On top of that, the civil service was politicised under Indira Gandhi. Because of the disintegration of the Congress party, and especially during the Emergency (compare chapter II.3.3), she had to rely 'on the civil service to administer and govern'. She closely worked with bureaucrats of her liking and 'retired the less pliant or exiled them to the Districts' (Khilnani 2004: 92). Khilnani evaluated that

> 'the independence and self-confidence of the civil service was weakened, as senior positions were put in the gift of political leaders' (Khilnani 2004: 89).

Consequently, the reasons for corruption within the bureaucracy are not only about regulative power, lack of accountability, administrative hurdles and economic scarcity, but also of a political nature:

> 'Corruption at the political level goes hand in hand with corruption at the bureaucratic level. … Political corruption has invariably resulted

into a sustained and systematic politicisation of the bureaucratic structure. It has liquidated the command and control structures of the services, leading to indiscipline, inefficiency and unaccountability among the ranks. Being used as tool for executing unlawful orders and as agents to collect funds for their political masters, a progressively growing number of employees ... have amassed fortunes through corruption. As a result ... the law-enforcing agencies have got mixed up with the very elements whose unlawful activities they are supposed to check and control. As the latter enjoy the patronage and protection of politicians, a frightening triangular nexus has evolved between criminals, government functionaries and politicians' (Bawa & Jain 2003: 35).

Because of the quota reserved for them in public jobs (see footnote 9 in chapter II.2), applicants from backward and scheduled castes and tribes could obtain almost twenty percent of the jobs in the bureaucracy since Independence. However, most of the officials with a rural background and those belonging to lower castes or classes 'seem to be largely relegated to clerical and other lower-level jobs in the administration', while higher civil servants tend to have upper caste backgrounds and are mostly of urban origin. Therefore, within the civil service, 'social hierarchy and administrative hierarchy seem to reinforce each other' (Pavarala 1996: 30).

The top position in the bureaucratic hierarchy is occupied by the Indian Administrative Service (IAS) and the Indian Police Service. Other central union services, such as Postal, Customs, Excise and Revenue Services follow and the individual state's civil services are at the last rung of the ladder.

Applicants who want to join the All-India Services have to compete in nationally held examinations between the age of twenty-one and twenty-eight. If they are successful in the subsequent interview, thereafter they first 'undergo extensive socialization in an initial training programme' (Pavarala 1996: 29) at the National Academy of Administration in Mussoorie.

'It is during this training that the officers are imparted the appropriate administrative ethos as well as sense of their superior social status' (Pavarala 1996: 29).

Thereafter, an IAS officer is assigned to a particular state, in which he starts his work at the District level, 'where the top civil servant is variously called a Collector, District Officer, or a Deputy Commissioner'. To promote a nationalist orientation among the bureaucrats and as a safeguard against vested interests, 'the practice has been to limit the number of (All-India Services) officers who serve in their state of origin to no more than 50 percent' (Pavarala 1996: 29).

It is important to mention, that all officials are transferred at least every three years. The higher the rank, the further away an officer can be posted, but generally no one is eligible to go to his home District, Subdistrict or Block (Gupta 2005: 9). The functioning of the bureaucracy and the administrative units will be explained more in detail in the case studies where they are relevant (see chapter III.2.2).

III.2.2. Bureaucrats & Corruption: Case Studies

In order to understand, under what logic and pressures bureaucrats operate from an empirical perspective, I will introduce three case studies in the following chapters.

In the first case study, Gupta (1995) sketched two Land Agents' encounter with two inexperienced young men from the village. His study focused on performative aspects involved in corruption. Thereafter, we will look at two officials responsible for controlling an innovative government scheme for rural development under which the money is directly given to village Headmen, not to bureaucrats, as in the past (Gupta 2005). Here we will get a first idea about the competition and mutual dependence which exist between bureaucrats and politicians, a topic at which we will look more in detail in the next case study of Wade (1982), in which he sketched the 'system of corruption' in irrigation; how prices are fixed and who profits. Wade says that a considerable sum of the money officials take actually goes towards higher-ranking politicians, because they are in charge of bureaucrat's transfers.

III.2.2.a. How two Land Agents Collect Bribes

This chapter draws on research by Akhil Gupta from 1984 to 1985 and in 1989 in North India (like III.1.1.b). Mandi is the pseudonym Gupta used for the administrative centre closest to the village he studied, where he observed the following encounter between bureaucrats and two young villagers. Gupta (1995: 378) described the public offices in Mandi as follows:

> 'Typically, large numbers of people clustered in small groups on the grounds of the local courts, the District magistrate's office, the hospital, or the police station, animatedly discussing and debating the latest news. It was in places such as these, where villagers interacted with each other and with residents of the nearby towns, as much as in the mass media, that corruption was discussed and debated.'

The office which we are concerned with belonged to the Patwari. A Patwari is a low-ranking, yet important (Gupta 1995: 378) bureaucrat who keeps the land record of five to six villages, about 5000 plots. He registers the land, sometimes even physically measures it and evaluates its quality. In order to prevent disputes about inheritance, he also records all deaths and births in land-owning families. A number of the Patwari's superiors are also responsible for the land records, so that there are, on an average, two officials for each village. Land is, as we should keep in mind, of vital importance to villagers, because it is 'the principal means of production in this setting' (Gupta 1995: 379).

Sharmaji, the Patwari in question, conducted his work in one of the basement rooms of his house. Another, lower ranking, Patwari called Verma was always with him. He

> 'functioned as Sharmaji's alter ego, filling in his ledgers for him, sometimes acting as a front and sometimes as a mediator in complex negotiations over how much money it would take to 'get a job done', and generally behaved as a confidant and consultant who helped Sharmaji identify the best strategy for circumventing the administrative and legal constraints on the transfer of land titles' (Gupta 1995: 379).

Sharmaji mostly sat on a small platform at the back of the room and talked with everyone. There were mostly two to three parties present and everyone joined the discussion. Most clients wanted to add or delete a name on the land title, divide up a plot or settle a dispute over ownership of farmland. They had to pay bribes in order to get these jobs done, 'but in most cases the rates were well-known and fixed' (Gupta 1995: 379). But still,

> 'however open the process of giving bribes and however public the transaction, there was nevertheless a performative aspect that had to be mastered' (Gupta 1995: 379),

as the following case study will illustrate.

One afternoon, when Gupta arrived at the office in order to do participant research, two young men had come to see Sharmaji in order to have a name added to the title of their plot (Gupta 1995: 379). The anthropologist was told that the young men wanted to have the name added to the list in order 'to obtain fertiliser on a loan on which the land was to serve as a collateral'. They were in their late teens, wearing rubber slippers and unkempt hair and their clothes had not been stitched by a tailor, as clothes worn by more distinguished town-dwelling young men. Both were somewhat nervous, which they tried to conceal by 'adopting an overconfident tone' in the discussion that followed. When Gupta came, the boys had already decided not to 'rely on Verma's help in getting the paperwork through the various branches of the bureaucracy', but to do it on their own. Sharmaji aggressively told them to go ahead and try and to come back if their attempts failed. One of the other farmers, who was anxious to get his own work done, told the young men that Sharmaji was well-connected and he himself added that even 'big farmers and important leaders' came to him for help (Gupta 1995: 380).

> '[P]erhaps because they had been previously unaware of his reputation, the nervous clients seemed to lose all their bravado. They soon started begging for help, saying 'Tau (father's elder brother), you know what's best, why should we go running around when you are here?" (Gupta 1995: 380).

Sharmaji instructed Verma: 'Help them get their work done' and Verma replied: 'I never refused to help them.' After a whispered conference next-door, Sharmaji reappeared and 'announced loudly that they would have to 'pay for it''. When they asked him, how much, Sharmaji answered: 'You should ask him [Verma] that'. But the latter also refused to name a sum. Instead he said: 'It is not for me to say. Give whatever amount you want to give.' When one of the boys handed him ten Rupees, however, Sharmaji burst out laughing and Verma smiled and said: 'I'll be happy to do your work even for 10 Rupees, but first you'll need the signature of the Headman of your village, that's the law' (Gupta 1995: 380). Sharmaji added that

> '*they didn't know anything about the law*, that it took more than 14 Rupees just for the cost of the application because in order to add a name to the plot, the application would have to be backdated by a few months' (Gupta 1995: 380, my italics).

When Verma mentioned the Headman of their village, the young men became nervous. They explained that they were not on good terms with him. Gupta had the feeling that Verma had anticipated this. Sharmaji then sent the boys away to find out about the 'going rate' for the transaction:

> 'Go and find out about the cost of putting your name in the land register, and then give Verma exactly half of that' (Gupta 1995: 380).

Before leaving for lunch with Verma, Sharmaji turned to one of the peasants present and asked him how much he had paid ten years ago. The farmer answered that it had been approximately 150 Rupees. The young men also asked the other clients present, all of whom said that it had been 130-150 Rupees ten or more years ago, but no one was able or willing to tell them about the present rate. The Patwaris had left, but as Gupta concluded, they knew that the young men

> 'would eventually be back and would then have to pay even more than the going rate to get the same job done' (Gupta 1995: 380).

Whereas the above example has focused on the encounter between clients and officials, the next case study will focus on the interaction between bureaucrats of different ranks supposed to oversee the correct use of development funds by village Headmen.

III.2.2.b. Inspecting a Development Scheme

From 1991 to 1992, the same anthropologist Gupta did research in the office of the Integrated Child Development Service and a Block Office[25], 'which coordinated the implementation of approximately 30 development programs' (Gupta 2005: 10).

The Block Office, in which Gupta conducted his research, had 20 employees and was headed by the so-called Block Development Officer (BDO). His assistants were in charge of sections of the development administration, such as agriculture, village governance (Panchayats), cooperatives, statistics, industry, service and business. There was one Junior Engineer for Minor Irrigation and one for rural employment schemes, with which this chapter is concerned. The other bureaucrats 'performed clerical duties'. All officials were transferred at least every three years, often sooner, as is the standard in the Indian bureaucracy (Gupta 2005: 9). Gupta evaluated the role of the Block office staff as follows:

> 'The Block staff played a relatively important role in the relation between the state and the rural population. For many villagers, the Block staff constituted the state's most regular representatives. However, they were not necessarily the state's most *important* representatives. That role probably belonged to electricity officials, the police, and the Patwari' (Gupta 2005: 10-1).

The incident I want to relate is the visit of two engineers employed by the District, Mr. Das and Mr. Chowdhury, who came to inspect the work done under the Jawahar Rojgaar Yojana (Jawahar Employment Scheme[26], abbreviated JRY). The scheme was initiated in 1989 by 'streamlining and combining all existing employment programs into one'. In 1994 5, JRY was the

---

[25] Mandi Block (a pseudonym) in Uttar Pradesh, was established in 1961 and had a population of just over 130,000 people in 89 villages thirty years later. 42 percent were Scheduled Caste and the modal (most frequent) village size was between 1000 and 2000 people (Gupta 2005: 10). In administrative terms, two to four Blocks like Mandi add up to one Subdistrict (Tehsil) and four Subdistricts together constitute the District, which in this case was headed by the District Magistrate, a junior official from the Indian Administrative Service. Altogether, there were 63 Districts in the state of Uttar Pradesh (Gupta 2005: 9).

[26] JRY was already briefly introduced in chapter III.1.1.a. Please note that the two authors used different transcriptions of the name of the scheme.

largest government programme for rural development in India, absorbing half of the money spent in this sector. Each village was allocated money depending on the number of inhabitants. This money was to be spend to improve the rural infrastructure by employing agricultural labourers for construction and maintenance of roads and other community assets such as drains and hand pumps or village ponds, during the troughs in the agricultural cycle, when many were unemployed (Gupta 2005: 10-1). The innovation about the JRY scheme was that funds were directly released to village Headmen, without being channelled or supervised through the bureaucracy – explicitly in order to reduce the opportunities for corruption:

> 'In a famous statement authorizing this change, former Prime Minister Rajiv Gandhi complained that most of the resources for development were being lost because of bureaucratic corruption, so much so, that less than 10 percent of the funds were reaching their intended recipients' (Gupta 2005: 10).

Theoretically, a meeting of all villagers should decide which projects were to be financed by JRY funds. In practice, meetings were only organised in villages with a weak Headman or where the Village Council was split. Mostly, the Headmen simply decided on the allocation of the money. The Junior Engineer of the Rural Employment Scheme was supposed to estimate the cost of the construction (Gupta 2005: 11). Usually, however, the money was given to Headmen without such an estimate. He could then 'do with it as he please[d]', because

> '[r]ealizing that most village Headmen were illiterate, the government decided to let them use the money as the Village Council decided, without burdening them with paperwork. It was felt that requiring Headmen to prepare estimates would once again give control of the process to literate bureaucrats. The Headmen just went ahead and started the work; when the money ran out, they stopped, even if the road was only partially constructed' (Gupta 2005: 12).

After the completion of the works done with JRY funds, the Junior Engineer was supposed to inspect and approve it. Thereafter, the second of three yearly instalments could be released. While this was meant to be a check on the Headmen, the official was pressured by superiors 'to ensure that the financial targets for the program were met':

> 'Although the Junior Engineer could hold up the subsequent release of funds, he was under a lot of pressure from higher officials to make sure that all the money ... allocated under the JRY for the District was actually used' (Gupta 2005: 11).

One day, Gupta went with the engineers Mr Das and Mr Chowdhury on a trip to inspect the works being done under the JRY. The Village Panchayat Officer (or 'Secretary', as he was normally called) accompanied them on their request. His job was to attend and protocol Village Council meetings in seven or eight villages allocated to him. In practice, however, as Gupta related, Secretaries and Village Headmen were often closely allied, so that each was free to act as he pleased. The Headmen did not have to bother with a procedural supervisor and the Secretary rarely visited meetings in 'his' villages (Gupta 2005: 12). Even though Secretaries were supposed to live close to their assigned villages, they seldom did and the usual practice was, instead, that Headmen needing a signature travelled to the town where the Secretary resided (Gupta 2005: 14).

The four of them started their drive towards the first village on a smooth road, which ended abruptly after a short distance and was followed by 'an extremely bumpy track' (Gupta 2005: 12). Mr Chowdhury said that he himself had been in charge of the construction of this particular road and he complained that

> 'he had asked for funds from the District Council, but the chairman of that body was far too busy *bestowing favors on villages that had supported him in his election and villages where he had friends and relatives* to pay him any heed. The dirt road, Chowdhury explained, had been unable to withstand the rainy season, hence its present condition' (my italics).

In both villages which they visited on that day, neither the Headman nor any Village Council members were ready to receive them. Their families and other villagers claimed not to know their whereabouts or where they kept their registers or about the location of any new constructions in the villages. The Secretary had no idea either, obviously indicating that he had not even been to the villages before. The only thing he knew was that in the first instalment 7000 Rupees had been given to the Headman of the first village and 8000 Rupees to the Headman of the second village. The inspectors were thus left to wander through the village and to decide on their own which one of the village roads looked as if it might have been recently constructed or repaired (Gupta 2005: 13-4). In the second village, they found two roads which looked as if they had recently been worked on. With no one to guide him, Mr. Das simply 'decided that the second road was the most recently constructed one'. This road was 'much better laid and longer' than the road inspected in the previous village. After the physical inspection,

> 'Chowdhury asked the Secretary how much of the money allocated for the project had actually been spent on it. The Secretary replied, 'You

have seen it with your own eyes; what can I say?' Chowdhury did not wish to let go: 'You must have received something out of all this, some money for chai-paani (refreshments, [used to refer to bribes]).' The Secretary said, 'All I get is 50 Rupees here or 100 Rupees there, nothing more than that.' 'Oh, come, come', Das interjected 'don't tell us that. It doesn't matter how much you make, what matters is how much you think actually gets spent on these things.' The Secretary remained silent' (Gupta 2005: 15).

Afterwards, in the car, Das 'let the Secretary feel the whole brunt of his fury' and asked to be shown the Secretary's records, because, as he told him, it was obvious 'that he [didn't] come to these villages at all' (Gupta 2005: 16). The Secretary defended himself by explaining that he lived far away and mentioning that it took him hours on the bus to get to the rather inaccessible villages (Gupta 2005: 14, 16, 32).

Another reason for the inspector's fury was that they felt that villagers treated them disrespectfully. On the whole, state officials and villagers seemed to regard each other with contempt and distrust. Chowdhury and other bureaucrats told Gupta that the situation was so bad 'that they had to ask people even for a drink of water' (2005: 15). Many bureaucrats traced the villager's new attitude to the time when subsidies began and the state emphasized its developmental role. One lower-level official told Gupta:

> 'When I first joined (government service), people used to consider it an honour if I sat down in their house and had tea with them. Now, they will not even offer tea to you unless they feel they have something to gain' (Gupta 2005: 16).

The bureaucrat himself explained this as follows:

> 'The more educated a man becomes, the more selfish he gets. It was due to this that villagers no longer had any respect for state officials' (2005: 16).

As this example shows, there are many different pressures at work within the bureaucracy: the relation to – and competition with – colleagues (of different ranks) and the demands made by superiors, politicians and the public. The next case study will look at these interdependences in a different context and in a very systematic fashion.

III.2.2.c. Corruption in Canal Irrigation

Robert Wade studied the performance of two canal systems in South India between 1976 and 1981 during six periods of fieldwork which lasted between one and four months. Additionally, a detailed investigation was made of local irrigation organisations in thirty villages and he stayed in one of these villages for several months. Wade's paper draws a comprehensive picture of the mechanisms underlying the determination of 'rates' and earnings in corrupt exchanges and bureaucratic transfers and their interdependence. He did not intend to study corruption, but

> 'once some degree of trust was established, farmers often volunteered information about how much they had to pay to the Irrigation Department; and while one would discount their figures in one, two or three instances, the regularity in farmers' statements across many villages did suggest that something more than wild exaggeration or generalisation was involved' (Wade 1982: 291).

It is important to note that irrigation differs from other public services in that it is not redistributive between classes, but increases the profit of private agricultural investment and that an effectively functioning canal system cannot be operated nor substituted privately. Thus, it may be assumed that

> 'the collective interests of big farmers would seem to correspond rather closely with good performance by the canal bureaucracy' (Wade 1982: 288).

In the South Indian state studied, paddy, groundnut, hybrid sorghum and cotton were, in declining order, the main crops under irrigation. There were two irrigation seasons: the rainy season from June to December and the dry season from December to May. Four million acres were fed from canal-systems controlled by the state Irrigation Department, which also constructed and maintained small tanks as local reservoirs. The official water rates since 1978 were 41 Rupees per acre and season for paddy and 28 Rupees for non-paddy crops (Wade 1982: 289-291).

The Irrigation Department had several sections with overlapping jurisdiction, but different responsibilities. The section Wade studied was the Division concerned with Operation and Maintenance (O & M) of the existing canal system and the construction of new, small, structures (Wade 1982: 289, 322). Following Wade, I use the term 'officer' here to refer to supervisors and their superiors (Wade 1982: 289, 323).

Administrative Hierarchy (Wade 1982: 290)[27]
Government: Minister & Secretary for Irrigation
General Chief Engineer
CE – Chief Engineer
SE – Superintending Engineer (Circle)
EE – Executive Engineer (Division)
AE – Assistant Engineer (Sub-Division)
Supervisor (Section)
Field Staff: Foreman and Banker

Sources of Illicit Income: From the Works Budget
Each Division got an annual grant for maintenance work calculated per acre, plus irregular grants for 'special work'. This money was split into Sub-Division budgets. The Supervisors prepared estimates for work to be done in their Section and these were coordinated by the AE and approved by the EE. The works to be done were assigned to private contractors. As so-called 'savings on the estimate', 'by long-established convention', 17 per cent of the contractor's pay were held back: 8.5 percent thereof were 'kicked back' to officers and staff of the Division. The EE, the AE and the Supervisor each got additional 2.5 percent (sometimes, the AE got more and the Supervisor less) and one percent went to clerical staff and draughtsmen (Wade 1982: 292-3).

The EE's 'additional income': Additionally, money was made from 'savings on the ground', by using less work or material than called for in the estimates. The balance was split between the contractor and the officers, who got between half and two thirds. The interest of the officers was to ensure a minimum quality and to raise their share, while contractors wanted to raise their income (from which they often also had to pay the local MLA - Member of the state Legislative Assembly), without getting into trouble with inspecting authorities that might turn up. However, if 'supplementary works' had to be performed later on, the contractors could keep all the profit from

---

[27] Each O & M Division was in charge of 80,000 to 400,000 gross acres of irrigated land and normally employed 350 to 400 people altogether, 50 of which were clerical staff (Wade 1982: 289, 322). Ninety percent of the remaining employees were field workers (Bankers and Foremen) who had at most a high school education and earned 300 – 700 Rupees a month. Supervisors were responsible for 7,000 to 20,000 gross irrigated acres, an area called a Section and had a two-year post high school diploma in Civil Engineering. Their immediate superiors, Assistant Engineers (AEs) were in charge of Sub-Divisions of 30,000 to 100,000 acres and often had a university degree in Civil Engineering. They earned about 1,900 Rupees monthly. The Division itself was headed by an Executive Engineer (EE). Four or five Divisions together constituted a Circle and were headed by a Superintending Engineer (SE). Their superior was the Chief Engineer.

that work for themselves. Wade estimated that the 'total rake-off' to officers amounted to between 25 and 50 percent of the value of what was meant to be constructed. Figuring in internal distributive mechanisms, an EE, whose average annually salary was 28,500 Rupees got at least 260,000 Rupees ($ 32,500)[28] in additional income per year in the area studied (1982: 293).

Postings of EEs: To get one of the much sought after, because profitable, O & M posts in the first place, however, an EE had probably bribed the Minister, promised him to respect his wishes on who was to get major contracts and to meet his demands for more money during the tenure in order not to be transferred early. Depending on their relative attractivity and profitability (discussed in more detail below) posts acquired price reputations. According to the engineers, most of the money went to the Minister himself (who in turn would had to pay a significant amount of money for his election campaign – compare III.3.1) and the rest to party funds. An EE also needed the approval of the local MLAs. In order to get it, he normally promised them to respect their choice of contractors for minor works (Wade 1982: 304). However, EEs 'without influence', from a low caste or another state sometimes also had to bribe other MLAs and senior officials. The prices, as indicated above, varied in relation to the attractivity of the posting. For an EE post, the prices differed between 50,000 Rupees for a posting in the uplands, where agriculture was less productive and farmers more resistant to paying bribes and 3 to 4 lakhs Rupees (one lakh = 100,000) in the more fertile coastal delta.[29] In the example above, the EE had to pay approximately 100,000 Rupees for his posting plus 50,000 Rupees to the Minister and senior officials during the next two years, more during the run-up to an election. Overall, a net profit of (again, at least) 370,000 Rupees for a two-year term (= $ 46,250 or approximately $ 63 daily) remained (Wade 1982: 305).

Controlling the Contractors: When Supervisors prepared the estimates for a job to be done, they already notified the small to medium-sized contractor who, according to the EE's preferences[30], mediated by the AE, was supposed to get the job. While tenders had to be notified publicly, the designated contractor always got it. He sometimes had to tip his competitors, but none

---

[28] In the late 70s, eight Rupees equalled one Dollar.
[29] Three specific posts for Superintending Engineers in the political centre of the state were known to cost 12-15 lakhs, 38-48 times the average annual SE salary. The money, it was said, could be recouped easily within two years. Incumbents of these posts 'made millions' (Wade 1982: 324).
[30] However, when big projects were undertaken, bigger contractors got them and those turned directly to Ministers or MLAs to bribe them. Local MLAs also tried to use their influence over officials to give jobs to contractors on whom they depended for money and support at election times.

of them would have dared to get in the way of the EE's decision, as he was the only person in the Division authorised to pay bills.

> 'An uncooperative contractor simply [found] that his bills [were] not paid – part of the art of the EE [was] to decide which bills should be paid and when, in order to keep his contractors in hand' (Wade 1982: 294).

Often, EEs also joined business partnerships with contractors (Wade 1982: 295) or gave cheap loans to them in order not to be caught by the Anti-Corruption Bureau. An informant told Wade that the contractors were often no more than the EE's 'dummies'. The EE

> 'len[t] them money to do the works, they present[ed] him with their bills, he (legitimately) encashe[d] the bills at the bank and pa[id] them – and then direct[ed] the contractors what to do with 'his' portion of the funds' (Wade 1982: 294).

When the Minister asked the EE for money, the latter simply sent one of his contractors to meet the Minister's agent, as none of them would touch the money with his own hands.

Sources of illicit income: from the irrigators
While the AE and the EE often collaborated to alter the works budget, the AE was left to raise the remaining five percent of his budget, which he had to give to the EE, (plus his own profit and the cost of his new posting, which will be discussed below) on his own (Wade 1982: 295). In order to do so, the AE 'sold' water to the farmers. Even though most canals were not operated trough rotation[31] but continually flowed, officials could manipulate the water flow to some villages through opening or closing particular gated sluices – and patrolling them.

Sometimes a village whose land was at the end of the distributive chain did not get enough water and farmers approached officials for their help (Wade 1982: 295). As the areas under cultivation were officially zoned into areas for irrigated paddy, irrigated non-paddy and non-irrigated other crop[32], villages who did not want to abide by the rules, also approached officials for assistance. Thus, 'tens of thousands of acres per canal' were being irrigated

---

[31] Wade pointed out, that canal operation by rotation, which was introduced in some areas, significantly increased official's discretionary power and their ability to collect bribes. 'In implementation, the irrigation staff [made] the supposedly rigid turn system highly flexible, depending partly on price' (Wade 1985: 299).
[32] Discussing this topic, Wade stated that the 'the zoning itself not uncommonly [made] no ecological sense' (Wade 1985: 317).

unauthorisedly and the stiff financial penalties meant to be fined were not collected anywhere. In practice, farmers representing a specific village would approach the AE with a request for more water or the assurance of continuing irrigation in the coming season (in the case of out-of-zone agriculture). The AE would send them to see the Supervisor, whom he instructed on how much money to ask for. Some bargaining might take place, but always between the Supervisor (who would, of course, have to check back with the AE) and the farmers, as the AE took 'care never to be seen asking money of farmers'. Not uncommonly, however, the farmer's representative was himself one of the contractors who worked for the Irrigation Department. As Wade (1982: 296) indicated,

> 'between the AE or Supervisor and some of the contractors develop[ed] relations of special intimacy, in which the bargaining [would] be more direct and more surreptitious.'

The farmers of one village, who collected the bribe among themselves, often had to pay several thousands of rupees which they handed to a designated contractor. On top of that, they had to pay a much smaller sum to the Supervisor, the man on the spot, who

> 'ha[d] no power independently of the AE or the EE ... if his demands [were] in the farmers' opinion excessive they [might] complain to the AE or EE about him and they, ever watchful to maintain the hierarchy, [might] discipline him' (Wade 1982: 297).

<u>AEs raising money</u>: As the AEs were under pressure to collect money, they did not always wait for farmers to approach them (Wade 1982: 296). Instead, if they needed money, they made sure that farmers knew 'they might suffer if they [did] not offer a bribe' (Wade 1982: 297). One engineer commented that 'rumour mongering' was one of the tricks of canal operators[33].

> '[M]erely by rumouring a shortage, money [could] be raised. If farmers scramble[d] to increase their supplies, the rumour [could] be self-confirming. More generally, the point [was] that a good deal of revenue [could] be raised from farmers with little work on the part of irrigation staff, by rumours, threats (especially to cut off water for unzoned crops), and occasional appearances by officers in their jeeps along the canal' (Wade 1982: 300).

As the control of an official over the operation of the canal system was highly imperfect, he could often not guarantee farmers that they would get

---

[33] He was talking about the field staff, as no engineer admitted that he was taking money for himself.

what they paid for. In case he couldn't deliver on his promises, he simply told the farmers,

> 'that there [was] a general shortage, that he [was] helpless, that they [were] getting more than they would have got had they not [had] paid' (Wade 1982: 300).

The AE's 'additional income': In the area Wade studied, some villages almost never paid money for water, others paid only during severe droughts and yet others had to pay regularly. Most often, farmers paid once for an assurance that they would get water in the dry season plus special money for additional wettings according to the weather. Altogether, this might add up to a cost of 10-25 Rupees per acre and year. For out-of-zone areas, the price, might rise up to 50 Rupees, at the most. Since the area under the jurisdiction of an AE was more than 50,000 gross irrigated acres, we can safely assume that an AE earned at least 50,000 Rupees from the money paid by irrigators. Plus his 2.5 percent from 'savings on the estimate', 15,000 Rupees, and presumed that he could at least double it with 'savings on the ground', he would end up with an additional annual income of 80,000 Rupees ($ 10.000) on top of the official 23,000 Rupees (Wade 1982: 301-2).

Transfers: As we have seen, AEs in O & M earned a lot of money. However, exactly how much could be made depended to a significant extent on local circumstances. As mentioned earlier, farmers in the more fertile and intensely irrigated delta areas, for instance, were willing to pay much more than villagers in the uplands. Thus, there were more and less profitable posts in the O & M department. Likewise, in the Irrigation Department as a whole, Investigations and Design posts were the least profitable and while Construction posts[34] were better, they were still less profitable than O & M posts for AEs and EEs. Besides personal reasons such as living conditions, nearness to the native village and prestige, two main factors decided about the desirability of a post: How much money could be raised (from the budget and from the farmers) plus how safe it was (in O & M control was minimal). As the rules prescribed, officers had to be transferred within three years. Because O & M posts were much sought after, no one could expect to stay in the department for more than a few years during his career. Politicians and senior officers were in charge of transfers and while they could not influence promotions, which were based on seniority, they were 'able to obtain for themselves part of engineer's additional income by auctioning the transfer' (Wade 1982: 303-4).

---

[34] Because in the Construction units, it was normally the Ministers, CEs and SEs who controlled the processes and profits.

AE's transfers: For AEs, the sanctioning authorities for a transfer were the superior CE and the SE. In addition, the local MLAs were concerned about who would get the AE post, because he would control water supply to potential allies and enemies. In order to get a certain post, an AE would first contact his prospective EE, promising him to turn over 5 percent of his budget to him and pay additional amounts during his tenure as demanded, and then visit the local MLAs and give them, for instance, 10,000 Rupees each. Sometimes, he would also have to pay the CE. The total cost for an upland post might be 25,000 Rupees, again leaving a considerable net profit, which is, however, significantly lower than that of the EE.

Supervisors only sometimes had to pay for their transfer into an O & M Circle (5,000 Rupees), but not for subsequent transfers within O & M. It was enough 'to 'yes sir whatever you say sir' the EE and the SE at every opportunity' (Wade 1982: 306), because the Supervisors did not seem to benefit very much from the corrupt exchanges taking place as evidence given by farmers indicated. Superior officials, however, often said that their field staff were 'corrupt fellows'.

Grain gifts, regarded as a tip, not as a bribe by the villagers were regularly given to the field staff after the wet season's harvest. For them, this was the main source of extra income and amounted to the equivalent of two to three months' pay (600 – 2,100 Rupees). AEs and Supervisors also got grain gifts, which amounted to a value of one or two months' salaries (up to 3,800 Rupees – Wade 1982: 301, 323).

III.2.3. Bureaucrats & Corruption: Findings

In the following chapter, I will summarise the most important findings generated from the analysis of the case studies presented above and also draw on further literature to underline my points. The first three chapters will focus on what strategies bureaucrats of different ranks employ to extract illicit benefits. Those who deal directly with citizens demand bribes – the height of which is partly determined by market mechanisms – primarily by exploiting citizen's insecurity (compare also chapter III.1.2.d). Their superiors as well as politicians use their power to authorise transfers and expen-ditures to contractors, to extract part of that money for themselves. However, it is important to note, that offi-cials of the developmental state have to implement many different programmes and are severely under-staffed, a problem which the Good Governance agenda fails to consider appropriately, as chapter III.2.3.d argues. The following chapter will discuss the consequences of understaffing and corruption for the system as a whole, namely the malfunctioning of public services, which may again lead to more rent-extraction (in order to pay for private facilities). This is already one of the explanations for bureaucrats taking part in corrupt exchanges. The next chapter will look at further justifications. Last but not least, we will focus on means to reform the system and resist pressures which can be used by officials, however, at the risk of having to bear the consequences of being transferred to 'punishment posts'. In conclusion, I will hypothesise how bureaucrats attempt to make sense of corruption.

III.2.3.a. Prices, Performance & Insecurity

As mentioned above, irrigation is not redistributive between classes, but instead especially beneficial for large landowners. Therefore, it seems that the reasons for high levels of corruption and the related performance-constraints in irrigation cannot be sought in the divergent interest of the dominant rural class, as was one of the explanation offered for the failure of a number of public services in Palanpur (compare chapter III.1.1.a).

Here, a different explanation has to be found: The bureaucrats who are in charge of canal irrigation,

> 'have great discretionary power, they allocate big money for maintenance contracts; they are responsible for rationing a valuable input between competing users, who have (officially) to pay much less than they would be prepared to pay for it rather than go without; and the officials make decisions which impinge heavily on the political prospects of politicians and on the economic well-being of local communities' (Wade 1982: 288).

As the example of Irrigation Management suggests, corrupt exchanges can take place where bureaucrats have discretionary power over a service for which people are prepared to pay more than they officially have to.

The bribes demanded from villagers depended upon several variables: (1) Dependence: More money was demanded in the dry season, where farmers completely depended upon canal irrigation. (2) Scarcity : If there was a drought in the wet season, the competition for canal water increased and officials had to put in more work to be able to assure water flow to specific villages. (3) Legality: Out of zone irrigation, as mentioned earlier, was more expensive. (4) Quantity & Demand: Paddy was expensive, because it needed more water (Wade 1982: 297). Groundnut also cost more than other crops, because it had to be irrigated in late April and May, when supplies often ran short. (5) Discretion: Villages whose water supply could easily be cut off by officials had to pay more. (6) Ease of Operation: Vice versa, villages whose request for more water required more management input, also had to pay more. (7) Politics: If a village was known to be politically powerful, it had to pay less. 'In the extreme case, no engineer would insist on money from the native village of an MLA' (Wade 1982: 298). (8) Demand / Regional Conventions: Generally, delta farmers were willing to pay more, because agriculture in their area was more productive and canal irrigation in the area had been practised for more than a hundred years. When they moved to the uplands, where canal irrigation had been introduced rather recently, they often became 'price leaders' (Wade 1982: 305, 323).

As the above listing of price-determining factors suggests, a black 'water market' existed which can be explained partly by economic models (compare chapter I.4.2) and it might be adequate to say, as some definitions have put it, that through bribery, a market-centred logic is permeating into areas from which policy makers aimed to exclude it (compare footnote 5 in chapter I.3). However, although Gupta's statement that the rates for transactions in land in 'Alipur' were 'well-known and fixed' seems to support this reasoning, we have to keep in mind that the 'market' was a highly imperfect one, because clients lacked secure information.

The third and the first example showed, that bureaucrats extracted bribes from clients explicitly by exploiting this insecurity (which was, in the case of irrigation, deliberately created by spreading rumours), their lack of detailed knowledge about procedures and prices as well as their inability to manipulate the procedures on their own. Or, as Wade put it:

'Bribes are high where uncertainty is high' (1982: 314).

Furthermore, the exchanges were not direct, instead officials were careful not to ask for a specific sum of money. Wade observed that

'revenue-raising [was] not a matter for boasting – even AEs chatting among themselves in private would be wary of discussing their revenue-raising exploits' (Wade 1982: 312).

Instead, prices were haggled over indirectly, sometimes by making use of a middleman, who might himself try to extract some money (chapter III.3.3.e). The process of disguised negotiations reminded of a carefully staged drama:

'Sharmaji appeared in turns as the benefactor and the supplicant pleading with his colleague on behalf of the clients. Verma managed to appear to be willing to do the work' (Gupta 1995: 380).

As the bureaucrats insisted on not asking for a specific sum of money, it appeared as if

'giving the bribe became entirely a gesture of goodwill on the part of the customers rather than a conscious mechanism to grease the wheels' (Gupta 1995: 380).

As I said in the introduction under I.2.4, discussing the example of the former communist countries, corruption in India also has the effect of excluding those who do not know how to negotiate. As Gupta summarised,

> 'the 'practice' of bribe giving was not, as the young men learned, simply an economic transaction but a cultural practice that required a great degree of performative competence. When villagers complained about the corruption of state officials, therefore, they were not just voicing their exclusion from government services because these were costly, although that was no small factor. More importantly, they were expressing frustration because they lacked the cultural capital required to negotiate deftly for those services' (Gupta 1995: 380).

This is another reason why especially marginalised citizens tried to avoid encounters with the bureaucracy (compare chapter III.1.2.g). It also indicates that simplifying procedures and making rules – and rates – publicly known has the potential to increase citizen's self-esteem in their encounters with officials and thus reduce illicit extortion.

III.2.3.b. Procedural Power & Hierarchy

Higher-ranking Bureaucrats in Irrigation Management were able to obtain most of the money lower-ranking bureaucrats extracted, because they had the power of authorising expenditures (mostly the pay to contractors) and transfers (to be discussed in the next chapter). For lower-ranking bureaucrats in irrigation, who were also often of lower caste and class background than their superiors, it was thus essential to 'yes sir whatever you say sir' their bosses on every occasion. The lowest officials, the Field Staff, hardly benefitted from the corrupt exchanges taking place, as they had no power independent of their superiors. The latter, however, trying to shield themselves from blame, often said that their field staff consisted of 'corrupt fellows'.

In the second case study presented, the superior Controllers did not have control over the lower-ranking Secretary. They suspected him and the Headmen of misappropriating funds and were furious that they couldn't find any evidence against them. They told Gupta that the other four pairs of engineers who were also employed by the District to inspect the JRY scheme, never even bothered going to the villages,

> 'because they realized it was just a waste of time. ... Apart from verifying that the structure was actually built, and did not just exist on paper, there was little they could do. ... And on those few occasions when they did manage to catch a Headman for the blatant misappropriation of funds, the Headman managed to escape punishment by using his political connections' (Gupta 2005: 16).

But while one explanation for the inspector's fury is their frustration at their inability to do their job properly, Gupta offered a different one:

> 'Now that the money was being directly allocated to Headmen, higher-level officials like Das and Chowdhury were being cut out of kickbacks and payments altogether. But they suspected that Secretaries continued to benefit since Headmen still needed to get their signature to verify that decisions and expenditures had been made as reported. Chowdhury's harshness with the Secretary has to be interpreted in this light, as arising both out of suspicion and jealousy' (Gupta 2005: 15).

The Secretary seemed to be aware of the lack of procedural power held by the Controllers and did not act very deferential, as he did not really answer their questions.

The JRY scheme reduced the number of people who profited from illicit use of funds and placed the money into the hands of Headmen. The new scheme was 'the cause of much grumbling and dissatisfaction' among District officials (Gupta 2005: 11). Many informants judged that the new method was a mistake,

> 'because Headmen had neither the education nor the technical competence or managerial skills to make effective use of resources' (Gupta 2005: 17).

However, their assessment of the scheme was not 'an uninterested one' (Gupta 2005: 17), as their 'unofficial income', was severely cut short by the new directive (Gupta 2005: 11). Although villagers agreed with bureaucrats that Headmen were appropriating a substantial part of the JRY money, many thought that the scheme had several advantages in comparison with its predecessors:

> 'Although stories about the corruption of Headmen were widely shared among officials and villagers, there were divergent assessments of whether the JRY was a success or not. Many villagers, and even some state officials, were of the opinion that the JRY was better than the employment programs that it had replaced. ... Headmen's lack of familiarity with bureaucratic procedure, and their *greater accountability to the villagers on whose votes they depended for the next election*, at least ensured that they spent a larger proportion of the money on the village than officials ever did. And since the money was now allocated to each village, it made sure that funds were not, in contravention of the rules, taken from villages that had no political clout to those that were the homes of powerful politicians' (Gupta 2005: 19, my italics).

The topic of politician's accountability to voters will again be raised in chapter III.3.

III.2.3.c. Transfers

Politicians and senior officers were in charge of transfers and while they could not influence promotions (which depended on seniority – Das 2001: 124), nor collected bribes directly from villagers, they were

> 'able to obtain for themselves part of engineer's additional income by auctioning the transfer, and imposing additional demands as a condition of the successful bidder's not himself being transferred out before the normal term' (Wade 1982: 303-4).

This inflated the prices dramatically, because

> 'an AE or EE would during his tenure – which normally lasted about two years – naturally [sic] try to recoup the money he had to pay to obtain the post plus what he had to pay to senior officers and politicians plus his own profit and what he would have to pay to obtain his next post' (Wade 1982: 305).

The original idea behind the institutionalisation of frequent transfers was to limit official's involvement in local politics in order to prevent them from becoming corrupted (Gupta 2005: 10). A senior official supported this reasoning when he told Gupta (2005: 31) that

> 'in the first year in a new post, he felt 'free' to take decisions on the merit of the case. After that, he knew too many important people in the area and had too many 'obligations' to locally powerful people to exercise his own independent judgement'.

But on the other hand, there was also a negative impact of the frequent transfers: Most

> 'officials felt accountable not to the local population but only to their superiors and to the particular bureaucracy in which they were employed' (Gupta 2005: 10).

In fact, less profitable posts – where citizens were less willing or able to bribe, for whatever reason – were so undesirable that in poor and famine-struck Kalahandi in Orissa, for instance, they were often not filled at all, as Jayal reported:

> 'about one-third of the total official positions, especially those in educational and medical institutions, where opportunities for profiteering [were] limited, generally remain[ed] unfilled' (Jayal 2001 (2): 203).

As Wade reported, payment for entry into the irrigation services was not necessary at the time of his study, as there had been a general shortage of engineering graduates and diploma holders since the mid-1950s (Wade 1982: 204). However, when I visited India more than twenty years later, many informants reported that they expected to have to pay to obtain a desirable post in the civil services (Fels 2005), possibly because the educational situation improved considerably and there were now more applicants competing for jobs. However, compare chapter III.3.3.e for qualification.

There are, as might be expected, depending on the structural location of those interviewed, different evaluations of whether politicians or bureaucrats or a criminal nexus between the two is responsible for corruption in the services (Pavarala 1996: 225-232).

Politicians are often held responsible by bureaucrats, because they use the system of transfers not only to extract money, but also as a threat to non-compliant officials. This has the effect 'not only of appointing bright and honest officials to inconsequential positions (often referred to as 'punishment jobs'), but also of severely disrupting their family lives'. As Pavarala (1996: 93) related, there 'was ample evidence during the course of [his] study to suggest the prevalence of such politically-motivated transfers' (compare Wade 1982: 309 for another example). Joshi and Mander asserted, that bureaucrats who tried to make a positive change were often punished.

> 'In India, the few progressive elements in the bureaucracy have often been marginalised. Bureaucrats who attempted to change things and took firm stands against corrupt practices have been routinely transferred out to 'punishment postings' and disempowered. Some attempted to change things in innocuous ways like setting right the system of records, but these exercises were centred around individuals and lasted only until the new entrant. The public remained at the mercy of chance benevolent administrators in the absence of institutionalisation of accountability mechanisms' (Joshi & Mander 1999: 25).

We will look at political corruption in section III.3 of the paper more in detail. Here we will only shortly look at the issue of rising transfer costs briefly mentioned in Wade's paper and speculate about what they might suggest.

As informants testified, the prices for transfers had risen considerably between 1966-68 because of intra-departmental conflicts which led to more involvement of politicians in transfer matters. In this case, senior bureaucrats as well as politicians were responsible for the rise in transfer costs. The second time, towards the end of the 1970s[35], after the electoral

---

[35] One particular postingthat had cost Rs. 30,000 in 1977 cost 100,000 in 1982.

defeat of the Congress party in the centre, which did, however, remain in control of our South Indian state, the local bureaucracy became an important means for raising money for the Congress. Here, it does indeed seem as if politicians were responsible for rising prices of transfers and the related increase in bribery. The prices rose again in 1981, possibly because a number of Construction Circles were surprisingly closed down, thus increasing the demand for O & M posts (Wade 1982: 306).

Although administrative changes are presided over by politicians, official's interest in earning substantial amounts through rent-extraction is also responsible for the rise of transfer prices. IWithout this interest, the whole 'system' of corruption in irrigation could not be sustained. A survey by the Lal Bahadur Shastri National Academy of Administration in Mussoorie in 1995 showed that 'one of the prime motives for joining the civil service was making money' (Sumita 1995, after Das 2002: 98). A survey in the Delhi administration reported similar findings. It revealed that 'the most sought-after posts involved public dealing, the departments with high budget outlay, and those which included issuing of numerous work contracts' (Arora & Goyal 1995: 632, after Das 2002: 98). A civil servant commented:

> 'I see that my juniors ... come with a single motto: *Jaldi paisa banao aur jao* (make money quickly and leave). ... They ask for a particular post, they lobby for it and are happy even if they get a short tenure in the seat (Das 2002: 98).

III.2.3.d. Good Governance & Scarcity

In his influential publication 'Asian Drama', Gunnar Myrdal argued in 1968 that officials' discretionary powers should be curbed and government needed to be reduced in order to curb corruption. In 1969, the subject was on the national agenda. As concerns about the abuse of public office and the criminalisation of politics grew in the 1970s and 1980s, the relevance of his calls was again highlighted (after Corbridge et al. 2005: 157). In the 1990s, Indian Prime Minister Narasimha Rao introduced a series of administrative and economic reforms. To control India's 'growing crisis of governability', as Atul Kohli had called it in 1990, he relied on a mix of deregulation, privatisation, civil service reform and decentralisation (after Corbridge et al. 2005: 158), as prescribed by the 'Good Governance' (and the earlier 'structural adjustment') agenda[36] promoted by the World Bank (chapter I.2.4).

---

[36] The involvement of consultancy firms like Arthur Anderson and Price Waterhouse Cooper and academic institutions such as the 'Harvard Centre for International Development' in formulating the new 'Good Governance' directives to restructure governments, has not yet received the attention it deserves, remarked Corbridge et al (2005: 153, 156).

However, the Good Governance agenda, as well as others who make mainly – or only – bureaucrats responsible for corruption, fail to take note of the

> 'contrasting and often competing pressures that are brought upon [bureaucrats]: from their seniors and communities of experts, for example, and pressures from important actors in political society, and perhaps even from some poorer 'clients', citizens and family members. ... the good governance agenda presupposes the construction of a type of individual that is uncommon in our field areas, and the manufacturing of which is hampered by a lack of state capacity. Government officers will find it hard to act like a Weberian bureaucrat if they lack the support of a Weberian bureaucracy' (Corbridge et al. 2005: 153).

As the Village Panchayat Officer in Mandi complained, it was difficult for him to travel to all the villages he had to cover. The engineers also complained that their inspections were not useful, because they lacked the time to investigate the spending of development funds in depth. They did not even have the opportunity to make out the Headmen or assert which structures had been built under the JRY scheme. Officials in irrigation also lacked capacity to effectively control all canals. Their only hope of maintaining a functioning system was the fact that villagers did not break gated sluices on their own, as long as they were confident that officials would meet their requests if bribed, and thus tried not to arouse their anger.

In their study 'Seeing the State. Governance and Governmentality in India', which draws on research projects carried out in five rural eastern Indian villages between 1999 and 2001, Corbridge et al. looked at the developmental state's understaffing in a more structured way and witnessed that many Block Offices in Bihar were simply overburdened. In 1999, a Block Office was required to administer, often in a 'decentralised' manner, six to eight times the funds it had received twenty years earlier, yet with about the same number of employees. A typical Block Office might be asked to run 100-120 schemes under the JRY programme detailed earlier (compare chapter III.2.2.b) and the newer 'Employment Assurance Scheme' (EAS), provide 1,000 houses under the Indira Awas Scheme[37] (compare chapter III.1.1.b) and construct 500 wells under the 'Million Wells Scheme' (Corbridge et al. 2005: 164). In one of the Blocks they studied, these schemes were supposed to be spread across fifty-five villages, many of which were difficult to reach. In another Block Office, which had 141 villages to cover, the administration was manned by the Head Assistant, an Accountant and two Assistants only. The technical staff consisted of two Junior Engineers and an Assistant Engi-

---

[37] Please note that different authors use slightly different transcriptions for the Indian terms.

neer, while the field staff ran to twenty-nine Panchayat Secretaries and nine Village-Level Workers. The Block Development Officer

> 'despaired of the situation. He told [the research team] that the better able and connected of his workers were trying to find work in urban areas, and that his accountant was not up to the task of handling cash transactions in the sum of Rs. 3-4 crores[38] (about $ 800,000 at 1999 prices)' (Corbridge et al. 2005: 165).

In a third Block, two Junior Engineers had to handle 300-400 schemes. For each of these, they were supposed to prepare estimates and layouts, work with the contractor, personally supervise the most crucial stages of construction, inspect and measure the progress to assure the flow of further funds and assist senior engineers in their inspection visits.

> 'Naturally, these tasks could not be completed properly, even where the Junior Engineer was working to the best of his ability. If there is state failure – and significant leakage of funds – it is at least in part because the local state is underdeveloped in relation to the tasks set for it' (Corbridge et al. 2005: 165).

Thus, while it may be true that some parts of Indian government and civil administration are overstaffed, this is not the case in Block Offices which have to implement a great number of development schemes. Rather, understaffing is a serious performance-constraint[39] (Corbridge et al. 2005: 165). Corbridge et al. concluded that

> 'money really does matter. It will be difficult to improve education or health care in eastern India when financial issues are easily discounted. .... There are doubtless efficiency gains to be made in government, and special interests to be confronted, but in eastern India the absence of a well-resourced public sector is what is most often noticeable. In some cases, the resources of the state have been looted by private interests as Harris-White describes in her account of ... Tamil Nadu. Government can then barely function, and ordinary men and women see the state mainly as an absence, or perhaps a phantasm. And when they see government officials they often see men (or women) who are very far from being the disinterested public servants in which the new public administration invests so heavily. In the

---

[38] One crore equals ten millions.
[39] Sub-Inspectors (SIs) of Primary Schools in West Bengal, also had serious capacity problems: One SI was responsible for 60-110 schools. However, the SIs only managed five to six inspections per month, because there was a shortage of clerical staff and vehicles (Corbridge et al 2005: 185).

lower reaches of government, especially, the pressures that are brought to bear on officials come far more from family and community, and from brute economic pressures, than they do from abstract models of the law or due process' (Corbridge et al. 2005: 185).

Thus, while it is local infrastructures of rule and the implementation of laws and development policies which need to be strengthened, the 'Good Governance' agenda, promoted by the World Bank and many other institutions, 'ever neglectful of political realities', once again points to privatisation and deregulation as the only remedies. Barbara Harris-White noted that the World Bank was missing two important points in its assessment, the first one being that tax evasion[40] is far more disabling of government than is corruption, and, the second one, that the state in India has de facto already been privatised to a great extent by local elites[41], as we could witness in Palanpur (chapter III.1.1.a). She concluded: 'The World Bank's project for the State is the opposite of what is needed' (Harris-White 2004: 100-1).

However, while the World Bank's analysis, as Leftwich formulated in 1993, is certainly

> 'naïve ... because it entirely ignores that good governance is not simply available on order, but requires a particular kind of politics to institute and sustain it', (after Corbridge et al. 2005: 186-7)

Corbridge et al. (2005: 186-7) defended it, saying:

> 'an intelligent defence of 'good governance' is that it is meant to *widen those* spaces of empowerment that can be found in a world of the second-best. ... It recognizes that the world is imperfect, and yet still open to contestation, and advances a politics of the possible which is expected to broaden the canvass on which a more committed pro-poor politics can be played out'.

I will look at and evaluate this idea later on, in chapter III.3.3.c and III.3.3.g.

---

[40] 'The evasion of tax is not only a matter of accumulative greed, it is also the most obvious sign of a distinctive conception of accountability and morality that focuses on close kin and immediate locality, and excludes the generation and redistribution of resources through the State to society as a whole' (Barbara Harris-White 2004: 100).
[41] 'Contemporary calls for the radical privatisation of the State ... ignore the effective radical privatisation, informalisation and now mafianisation that south Asian States have been undergoing for much longer than the era of liberalisation of the 1990s' (Barbara Harris-White 2004: 101).

III.2.3.e. Costs of Corruption

Wade pointed out that the bribes farmers had to pay to O & M officials were not high when compared to the profit from agriculture. While, for each acre of paddy, net profits were approximately 900 Rupees and pre-harvest costs for cultivation were also 900 Rupees, corruption costs per acre were commonly 10 to 25 Rupees over two seasons and often much less, certainly not more than 50 (Wade 1982: 314).

Thus, the main negative effect of corruption in this department was, as Wade (1982: 325) convincingly argued, not the illicit extortion from farmers, but 'savings' from the budget and its constraining influences on performance as a whole. The

> 'difference in the 'partial equilibrium' and 'general equilibrium' effects of the corrupt system in irrigation is similar to the probable effects of 'speed money' in the bureaucracy as a whole. Speed money, if common, probably has the effect of *slowing down the overall work performance* of the bureaucracy, as officials cut back their work effort in order to invite the payments of bribes, by means of which individuals are able to accelerate officials' effort from this reduced level to deal with their particular cases' (my italics).

However, as the previous chapter has shown, many Block Offices in Bihar were so seriously understaffed that they could not perform all their tasks appropriately, even if they wanted to. In that case, bribing them could be a means for citizens to get officials to turn their attention to their specific areas or problems.

In any case, the performance of public services suffers (as shown in chapter II.4 and looked into in chapter III.1.1.a), probably both because of understaffing and because of corrupt officials. This, in turn, often forces individuals to pursue private services, for instance, in education and health care. Kansal argued that the

> 'poor quality of education provided in the government schools has forced individuals to pursue private schools out of their financial reach. This further forces individuals in power to be more corrupt. This in a long run has divided our society in distinct educated and totally illiterate groups' (Kansal, 2001: 1).

We will look into this argument more in detail in the following chapter.

III.2.3.f. Political Pressures & Consumerism

Because none of the authors of the three case studies presented above, reported on how bureaucrats justified bribe-extraction or talked about bureaucrat's attempts to reform the system, this as well as the next chapter also draw on a different publication. Vinod Pavarala interviewed sixty members of the elite in Andhra Pradesh for his empirical constructivist[42] study 'Interpreting Corruption: elite perspectives in India' between 1989-1991. His interview partners included fifteen bureaucrats from the All-India Services (compare chapter III.2.1), eleven politicians who were elected members of the Andhra Pradesh State Assembly or top officials of political parties, twelve journalists, twelve judges and ten industrialists or business men (Pavarala 1996: 28-31, 41-3)[43]. When Pavarala asked his informants who was responsible for corruption in India

> 'a majority of the respondents readily named elite groups other than their own and individuals within them ... while many politicians held bureaucrats primarily responsible for corruption, the industrialists tended to blame both politicians and bureaucrats ... Similarly, many bureaucrats blamed 'the nexus' between politicians and industrialists, while many judges and journalists tended to name all the groups involved in this study other than themselves' (1996: 84-5).

The bureaucrats interviewed offered legalistic definitions of the phenomenon and while two-thirds suggested that corruption may help in promoting greater administrative efficiency, most also said that corruption had adverse effects on politics (without, however, threatening the legitimacy of the democratic system in general), created distortions in the development objectives of the state and had negative consequences for the economy[44]. Almost all of them identified politicisation of the bureaucracy, influence of money power in elections, low quality of political leadership as well as communalism and familism (elements of 'indigenous culture' – compare chapters I.4.1 and III.3.3.e) as primary causes for corruption (Pavarala 1996: 225-6), subjects which will be discussed in the next chapter.

---

[42] Pavarala locates his study within the perspective of 'contextual constructionism'. He looks at how elites construct their definitions and etiologies of corruption and makes sense of this information by contextualising it (Pavarala, 1996: 25).

[43] Most of the bureaucrats had an urban, upper-class or upper-middle-class background, but more than half of the politicians (while stemming from upper castes) had rural backgrounds and their families were agriculturalists. The journalists were editors, senior news editors or chief reporters of major newspapers published in Andhra Pradesh; the judges were retired chief justices of the state high court and current judges at both the district level and the high court and the businessmen were owners, chief executives or those immediately below them in the hierarchy of major private business firms or industries (Pavarala 1996: 28-31, 41-3).

[44] While younger bureaucrats thought that excessive state controls of the economy led to corruption, older ones, 'who seemed to have been socialized into the socialist agenda of an earlier era', defended the regulations.

There are many different pressures on officials, which are hard to stand up to. For officials in the Irrigation Department, Wade (1982: 309) summarised the situation as follows:

> 'It is clear, then, that the pressures on any one [bureaucrat] to behave in a 'corrupt' manner, whether in response to demands from superiors in the irrigation hierarchy or to satisfy the expectations of politicians and farmers, are very strong. Many engineers find the pressures to which they are exposed from all sides (especially on O & M jobs) very trying and find the behaviour needed to stay in the post in varying degrees distasteful. Morale in the Irrigation Department is certainly low. Why do not some of these individuals express their resentment at the way they are being treated by taking action against those who harass them, perhaps by complaining to the Secretary of Irrigation, or to the Anti-Corruption Bureau? In the words of an EE, 'I would be crushed, I have my family to support, so I just keep quiet" (Wade 1982: 309).

Besides the threat of being transferred to punishment posts if they displeased their political masters (compare chapter III.2.3.c), a majority of the officials suggested that low wages led to corruption (Pavarala 1996: 225-6). While all Pay Commissions, periodically set up by the government to suggest reasonable wage rates for government officials, agreed that officials should be given a 'living salary' from which they could sustain themselves and their families, it is debatable what a 'decent standard of living' is.

As officials often compared themselves to their counterparts working in private companies, the Fifth Pay Commission (1995-7) looked at enumerative differences in the sectors and concluded that 'it [was] indisputable that there [was] a yawning gap between the salaries and benefits available in the private sector and the government at all levels'. While it warned that 'this problem if not addressed … is likely to gradually spell a rot in the system. Not only is a flight of talent an immediate possibility, a tendency towards corruption is equally likely', it also acknowledged that it was 'constrained by the availability of funds within the government in making recommendations' (after Das: 102-7).

While wages for bureaucrats did not catch up with those in the private sector, a 'rising wave of consumerism' spread across the country since the 1980s when the government opened up the Indian market. A chief reporter of a newspaper in Andhra Pradesh asserted that people were 'hankering for commodities which were considered luxuries until recently, things like, refrigerator, color television, a music system, a scooter, a car' (Pavarala 1996: 114). A District judge put it this way:

'The honest man has become the butt-end of ridicule. In modern life, society is flooded with consumer goods, status symbols; if you don't have them, you are not even considered an individual. We have become an acquisitive society which regards a money-making machine as God. I didn't want to buy any of the stuff I now have, but because of society's pressure I took a loan from my provident fund and bought it. It would have been easier to get a hefty bribe from someone. There is so much of social pressure that it can be life-taking' (Pavarala 1996: 115).

Several of Pavarala's informants suggested that these pressures were especially high for those who had recently risen to the middle classes and started to mix with people in possession of 'old money'. Trying to keep up with their peers in a 'society like India, with its glaring disparities of wealth and status', many succumbed to corrupt pressures (Pavarala 1996: 116-8). What this implies is, that in settings in which inequality prevails, yet social mobility is on the rise, corruption may – at least temporarily – increase.

III.2.3.9. Morality & Reforms

However, there are also bureaucrats who resist the pressures and try to reform the administrative system. While it is difficult to assess whether a bureaucrat's testimony about his own integrity is trustworthy, it is nevertheless neither advisable to discount such a statement from the beginning. Harsh Mander, who wrote the paper on which chapter III.1.1.c is based, stated:

'Having served the bureaucracy for nearly two decades I know you are given so much legal protection and statutory protection, that if you stand up, all they can do to you is transfer you out. ... So there is space to stand up and be counted. I served more than 21 years. I don't think that even for a day I did anything my conscience told me not to do' (Phukan: no year)

When Harsh Mander was stationed as a Commissioner in Bilaspur Division (which belonged to the state of Madhya Pradesh, but lies in the newly formed state of Chhattisgarh today), he obliged ration shops to 'disclose the stocks and names of beneficiaries to anyone who desired to know'. This idea was later copied by the state government under Digvijay Singh and extended to other government departments (Phukan: no year).

In an article co-authored by Mander himself, the scheme is described more in detail[45]. The stated goal of his order was to introduce systematic transpa-

---

[45] Without, however, mentioning, that one of the authors himself was it's initiator.

rency in the Public Distribution System, the Employment Exchange and the Pollution Control Board. Mander ordered each ration shop to send certified copies of the Stock, Sale and Ration Card Register to the Tehsil[46] office. From there, any citizen was entitled to get certified copies of all these documents within 24 hours of inquiry. Delays by officials in handing out copies were fined. Similarly, the Employment Exchange had to give details about the merits and procedure of recruitment for applicants to any public position on demand (Joshi & Mander 1999: 27). The Pollution Board was ordered to publish pollution levels daily in the local press and a citizen's committee was trained to check the publications. The success became quickly visible. Although the number of information seekers was 'negligible',

> '[t]he foodgrain shops recorded unprecedented excess stocks, as the distributors could no longer oblige local politicians and goons by diverting the stocks to them and to the black market. They even remarked, 'the people's right to know has become our right to 'no'! Pollution levels showed a marked decline and the daily publication of pollution levels encouraged the public to take an interest in their environment and to question the levels of pollution' (Joshi & Mander 1999: 28).

This asserts the suggestion made in chapter III.2.3.a, that making procedures publicly known has the potential to reduce opportunities for bribe-extraction. However, as local leaders were unhappy about the new directives, the Commissioner was soon transferred out of the area. After his withdrawal, the whole system collapsed. While critics have therefore described the experiment as a failure and claimed that it was 'impractical' as well as 'financially infeasible',

> 'the ground had been well prepared and the seeds sown for sweeping acceptance of the right to information in principle in the entire state of Madhya Pradesh. Since this was an experiment carried out pro bono, it found many supporters who could look beyond the teething troubles and sense that here was an answer to many ills to which many cures had earlier failed. It was this realisation that spurred the Chief Minister of the state, himself a professed crusader for decentralisation of power and transparency and accountability, to attempt an enactment for enforcing the right to information' (Joshi & Mander 1999: 28).

The government 'asked the officials to enumerate all those categories of information which were easily available with them and which could be given without any extra burden on the administration' and then prepared executive orders for 37 departments of the state government[47], ordering

---

[46] A Tehsil or Taluk is a subdivision of the administrative District.
[47] For example: Public Works, Panchayats and Rural Development, Urban Develop-

them to hand out desired information to any enquiring citizen. However, as Mander and Joshi criticised, the orders were not systematically publicised, nor was there any concrete plan on how to inform and train bureaucrats with regard to the new orders.

> 'Interaction with some of the lower bureaucracy revealed that to them the implications of the directives on right to information had no relevance to public dealing and some even considered that these were meant to allow them access to their own service and leave records, etc.' (Joshi & Mander 1999: 31).

Another problem was that there was no system for enforcing the order and hence it 'lacked teeth' (Joshi & Mander 1999: 31). Several civil society groups 'initiated a campaign to educate people about the operation of the right and to activate the orders by filing applications for information'. They met with anything from 'dogged refusals to threats of physical harm'. Thus, they primarily focused on building awareness and civil society coalitions, held workshops and disseminated information about the new order, for instance, by distributing a pictured booklet (Joshi & Mander 1999: 32).

The example suggests that attempts at administrative reform meant to enhance accountability can be quite successful if they are given 'teeth' and political support and are used by the people. Their right to know can also empower bureaucrats to say 'no' to the demands of local leaders. However, it also shows, that reforms from above are met with the same level of resentment by implementing officers and politicians, as those from below. Higher-ranking bureaucrats can achieve changes simply by demonstrating that improvements are possible. Even if they are transferred out (compare chapter III.2.3.c), their work might continue to have an impact. However, they and their families might have to bear the consequences of being transferred frequently and accept to live from the official salary only. Additionally, they do not necessarily command respect among colleagues or politicians, as one of Pavarala's informants, a bureaucrat admired for resisting political pressures, complained. Speaking about a colleague, he said:

> 'This particular officer made about a million or one-and-a-half million rupees in a span of one year. Normally for an officer in the All-India Services, that is the amount one can make in an entire lifetime. Everybody knows he is corrupt. Only the morally upright think this is a bad fellow, but everybody else thinks he is great. People want him in their districts because he will oblige them ... He is in a cushy job now and is not treated as a black sheep or anything' (Pavarala 1996: 113).

---

ment, Dairy Development, the Public Distribution System, Jails, Social Welfare, Co-operatives and Tribal Welfare Forests.

III.2.3.h. Who Sets the Limit?

I suggest that social consensus sets the limit for rent-extraction. As the example of Irrigation Management shows, villager's willingness to pay determined levels of corruption. In areas were farmers were resistant to paying large bribes (in the uplands), postings were less costly and thus less money had to be raised from illicit earnings.

However, an important qualification is that this rule holds true only when talking about the *average willingness* to pay in an area. A single villager's resolve to pay less would have little influence on price levels. A new resident, who is prepared to pay more than the going rate, in contrast, can easily become price-leader. Thus, there is a classic dilemma: While it would be preferable for everyone, if farmers agreed to pay less bribes, in a bribe-giving environment it is to an individual's immediate advantage simply to pay the money and get on.

Villagers can defend themselves against rent-extraction by lower-ranking irrigation officials by appealing to their superiors, who are ever watchful to maintain the (administrative as well as social) hierarchy, but only if it is higher than usual or higher than what superior officials or locally influential leaders are willing to 'allow'.

If officials repeatedly don't keep promises given for taking bribes, villagers may lose their trust in the effectiveness of bribes, and, in the case of Irrigation Management, it becomes more likely that they break gated sluices to increase their share of water (Wade 1982: 323), something they usually don't do (at least not too often), in order not to incur the wrath of the irrigation staff, who might refuse to help them later on (Wade 1982: 296). This is a check on the extent to which an officer can collect bribes and give promises without delivering (Wade 1982: 323). As Wade summarised:

> 'The main check on the engineers comes from the farmers they are meant to serve. It is true that the farmers themselves are often willing partners to bribery; as we have seen, they will rush to pay if their crops are at risk, and they will, in some locations at least, be willing enough to pay for water for unauthorised irrigation. However, if an engineer comes into a post and starts demanding significantly *more* from farmers and contractors than was usual previously, then they may try to take action to check or avoid his demands. They may in some locations break the channel banks or sluice-gates to by-pass his control ... and/or visit their MLA. ... But this mechanism is limited to the extent that farmers fear that the engineer and local staff will strike back at them. ... It is also limited by differential willingness of MLAs to act. ... in the complacently-spoken words of an AE: 'Villages of small

farmers just have to suffer, they won't dare approach Ministers or MLAs" (Wade 1982: 311).

However, if villagers seriously challenge the system of corruption as such, like in chapter III.1.1.c or the example above or by refusing to pay bribes, they run into serious trouble with leaders and authorities, which they can only override, if they are well organised and supported. In Kalahandi, for example, where tribals hardly bribed officials, simply because they could not afford it, many public posts remained empty (compare chapter III.2.3.c). Since villages where powerful leaders come from, often do not have to bribe at all, it becomes evident that political power is a competitor and controller of bureaucratic power. This seems like a good sign, because politicians, as mentioned in the evaluation of the new JRY scheme, can at least be held accountable through elections.

The newly developed 'disrespectful' behaviour towards higher-ranking officials which Gupta's informants complained about (see chapter III.2.2.b), might be an indication that villagers felt empowered vis-à-vis bureaucrats by the new JRY scheme and thus openly showed their contempt of presumptuous officials. As reported above, one of the officials blamed the villager's unwillingness even to offer them a glass of water, on rising levels of education. As Gupta remarked:

'Since state officials often derided villagers for their 'illiteracy', this unselfconscious reference to the correlation between education and selfishness was particularly telling. The subtext of this statement was that education had so emboldened them to think of themselves as being equal to officials that they no longer displayed an appropriately deferential attitude towards them' (Gupta 2005: 16).

III.2.3.i. Bureaucrats Making Sense of Corruption

In summary it can be said, that the pressures upon an individual bureaucrat of the developmental state machinery can make it difficult for him not to become corrupt. His job is difficult and his office often understaffed, while his salary is low and he typically has to support a family from it, maintain class standards, pay for private schools, health care etc. His local power can also be quite limited and he can't easily afford to get into the way of superiors and politicians who all accept to receive their share of his corrupt earnings. If he refuses to take part in corrupt dealings, he might be transferred to an undesirable post, maybe in an inaccessible location. Thus, even while some bureaucrats themselves despise of rent-extraction and prefer not to talk about it even with each other, they often seem to succumb to pressures, viewing corruption either as a hard-to-dispel necessity or as a money-making opportunity they might deserve since their job is so difficult. Others, however, resist or are at least willing to do so once they are supported from outside, that is from citizens and/or superiors. It is significant that some bureaucrats in Madhya Pradesh stated that the citizen's power to know became their right to say 'no' to the demands of local grandees.

III.3.1. Political Players' Quest for Influence

As the first case study presented in this paper showed (compare chapter III.1.1.a), those villagers in Palanpur with some 'influence' paid less or no bribes to obtain state services. In chapter III.2.2.c, it was established, that those villages where politicians came from, did not have to pay bribes for canal irrigation. On top of that, many of the bureaucrats interviewed by Pavarala assigned responsibility for corruption to politician's involvement in bureaucratic matters (see chapter III.2.3.f). Therefore, I hypothesised that the quest for political influence is important to look at when analysing the phenomenon of corruption. The aim of this final part of my study, after giving a brief general introduction to Indian politics, is to investigate to what extent politicians actually control bureaucrats and citizens (and therefore, the use of state funds) and who checks their power.

III.3.1. Introduction to Indian Politics

As Weiner stated,

> '[w]herever there is power, there must be politics – a law as fundamental in political sciences as supply and demand is in economics' (Weiner 1967: 167, quoted after Robinson 1988: 54).

Following him, I will not limit the following chapter to looking at professional politicians only. Rather, I want to investigate local power relations in three different settings by looking at all the actors, bureaucrats, politicians and ordinary citizens alike, who are involved in competing for control over state resources and fellow villagers.

As discussed above, considerable power in India is vested in bureaucrats. Likewise,

> 'political power in India, as in many other countries, has been an important road to obtaining wealth and status in society. The domination of the state in the national economic scene enables political elites to garner critical socio-economic resources and distribute them differentially. Members of Parliament (MPs) and Members of the Legislative Assemblies (MLAs) enjoy considerable perks for a country like India. These include travel and other allowances, cars, government housing, telephones, and medical care. They use these facilities and their posi-

tion in the power structure to distribute patronage to political supporters, friends and family' (Pavarala 1996: 38-9).

The state does not fund elections. Rather, politicians and parties have to raise money from their supporters and theoretically list all contribution of 20,000 Rupees and more for audit. Because elections have become very competitive and thus expensive[48] (as new groups have entered the competition – Khilnani 2004: 54), 'the emphasis in each party seems to have shifted from honesty to capacity to raise funds', analysed Bawa and Jain in their study for Transparency International (Bawa & Jain 2003: 21). Besides corruption, other illicit methods of winning elections have been employed by aspiring candidates:

> 'The compulsion to win power publicly and legitimately has provoked unpicturesque illegalities, old and innovative – violence, corruption, and 'booth-capturing" (Khilnani 2004: 58).

In some instances, criminals, employed by politicians to intimidate citizens so that they would vote for them, have abandoned their 'masters' and instead 'campaigned' for themselves. Thus, 'dacoits and criminals' have entered politics, as Brass (1997: 308) complains. However, as will be evident from the first case study to be presented, violence has long been used in politics and it could easily be argued that those who order the beatings are more criminal than those who obey them to earn their living.

Khilnani (2004: 51), talking about secessionist movements within the federal Indian state, argued that centralism was responsible for the rise of regionalisms which led to violent clashes. However, 'in spite of the great power vested in the central government by the Indian Constitution', the state governments also hold considerable power. They are in charge of law and order, justice, agriculture, irrigation, education, public health, industries and land rights. In most states, there is a single, directly elected assembly.

> 'As the state government is a significant source of patronage, there is intense intra-elite competition to obtain elective positions at the state level and the role of money power in the campaigns compare with that in the general election' (Pavarala 1996: 39).

After the Green Revolution, which 'substantially improved the economic power of owners of large and medium-sized landholdings', many farmers have entered politics, especially in the states. Pavarala argued that,

---

[48] In the South Indian state in which Wade studied the performance of canal irriagtion it was said 'that a man need[ed] to have at minimum one lakh [100,000] rupees available before it [was] worth even thinking about contesting an MLA's seat' (Wade 1982: 319).

> 'a major consequence of this social composition of politicians [was] the infusion of a feudal political culture, with scant respect for modern democratic institutions and a strong penchant for the personality cult and sycophancy' (Pavarala 1996: 40).

Corbridge and Harris, following Austen (1993: 13, after Corbridge and Harris 2000: 200), interpreted it differently. They argued that two transfers of power within India had already taken place: from the British to the Indians first and thereafter from feudal lords, who were often urban-based, to larger, village-based, peasants. The third transfer of power to the subaltern masses had not yet been accomplished. Yet,

> 'the poor [we]re becoming ever more involved in India's politics and ... [we]re pushing hard for a greater share of state resources ... the deepening of democracy in India offer[ed] India's 'social majorities' their best hope for taking some control over the economic and political structures which govern[ed] their lives and which might yet be made to work for their empowerment' (Corbridge & Harris 2000: 239).

While many proponents of the Good Governance agenda point to civil society as a site for empowerment, Corbridge et al. emphasised that,

> 'for poorer men and women, especially and indeed for many government employees ... the state [wa]s sighted in large part through the lens of political society' (Corbridge et al. 2005: 187).

I agree with them that

> [w]e need to pay close attention to those sightings' (Corbridge et al. 2005: 187).

III.3.2. Politics & Corruption

Politicians are at least as unwilling as bureaucrats to admit to taking bribes and it is probably even more difficult to gather information about their illicit dealings. Therefore, there is no empirical investigation focusing exclusively on political player's corruption. However, there are case studies which analyse local power configurations more generally and occasionally touch on the subject of corruption, and three of these will be introduced. The relation to the topic of this thesis will be elaborated mainly in the following discussion of the findings, drawn from a comparison of the case studies as well as further literature and taking into account the results generated so far. The first case study adds a historical perspective to our discussion and is taken from a political monograph about a village in Andhra Pradesh written by Marguerite Robinson and published in 1988. In my summary, I will focus on the change in local power relations that occurred since the seventies and on the factors which shaped this process and undermined the near-total control of wealthy landowners over other villagers.

Thereafter, I will present a combined introduction to the following two (as well as three other) case studies taken from Corbridge et al. (2005). In the village in Bidupur Block in Bihar, the power of local patrons is so far-reaching that the local District Magistrate not long ago still surrendered most of the development funds directly to local politicians. These used the money for development schemes in the villages of their supporters. In West Bengal, in contrast, villagers participated in political decision-making. Politicians from a diversity of backgrounds, also poor and low-castes ones, had replaced the leadership roles formerly played by big landowners and morales were quite high.

III.3.2.a. Political Change in Andhra Pradesh

Marguerite S. Robinson's study of political development in a village in Andhra Pradesh covers the period from 1957-81. She first visited 'Mallannapalle' (a pseudonym) in 1969. In 1971-2, she lived there for ten months and since then made short visits nearly every year (Robinson 1988: xi).

The administrative structure, like elsewhere in India, consisted of three layers: Village Officers (Patels), the Tehsildar responsible for several villages and the Collector[49], who supervised the District. With the Indian-wide introduction of 'Panchayati Raj', that reduced the powers of officials, the further administrative unit of Community Development Block[50] was established for planning and executing development schemes. The senior official at this middle level was the Block Development Officer (BDO), who supervised a staff of technically trained officers.

---

[49] Who is an IAS-officer, see chapter III.2.1.
[50] In Nasarpur, Taluk (the area over which the Tehsildar resided), Community Development Block and Legislative Assembly constituency were isomorphic; this is often not the case.

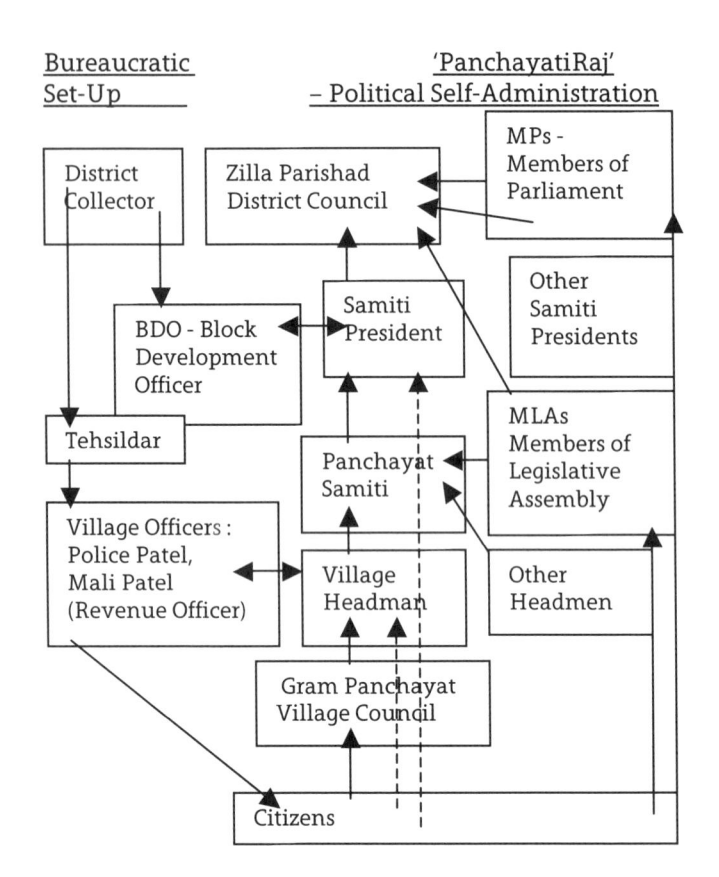

Bureaucratic Set-Up	'PanchayatiRaj' – Political Self-Administration
District Collector	Zilla Parishad District Council — MPs - Members of Parliament
BDO - Block Development Officer	Samiti President — Other Samiti Presidents
Tehsildar	Panchayat Samiti — MLAs Members of Legislative Assembly
Village Officers: Police Patel, Mali Patel (Revenue Officer)	Village Headman — Other Headmen
	Gram Panchayat Village Council
Citizens	

The first level of Panchayati Raj (Political Self-Administration) consisted of the Village Council, the Gram Panchayat[51]. One member (Panch) was elected for every one hundred and fifty villagers. These Panches then elected the village Headman called Sarpanch (after 1981, he was directly elected by the people and the power of the Panches decreased drastically – Robinson 1988: 50-1, 237). The Sarpanches and the Member of the state's Legislative Assembly (MLA) for the region and a few appointed members formed the Panchayat Samiti which functioned at the level of the Block. In 1972, the Nasarpur Panchayat Samiti consisted of sixty-three Sarpanches, the MLA and six co-opted members.[52] Theoretically, the assembly made policy decisions concerning development and the BDO and his staff had to implement

---

[51] Villages with less than a thousand inhabitants were grouped together to form a single Gram Panchayat (Robinson 1988: 50-1, 237).
[52] At that time, the members of the Panchayat Samiti elected their own president (after 1981, he was also elected directly by the people).

98

them. However, the division of power between the President of the Panchayat Samiti and the BDO depended on their qualifications and the support each could muster and thus varied from region to region and over time. In Nasarpur, the Samiti President was usually more powerful and played an important role in the implementation of (his own) policies.

At the third level, the Samiti presidents, MLAs and Members of Parliament (MPs) from the District plus a few state-appointed members formed the Zilla Parishad, the District Council. In contrast to the situation at the Block level, District officials were not subject to the authority of the political Zilla Parishad. In Andhra Pradesh, the latter institution was an organisation with little power[53] (Robinson 1988: 50-3, 237).

Since the early twentieth century, two families of the Reddy cultivator caste had dominated the village Mallannapalle. Srinivas had held the then hereditary office of Police Patel, but lost his power in the fifties[54]. Pratap Reddy was the Mali Patel (Revenue Officer). His brothers Lakshma and Narasimha lived jointly and the latter was the Village Headman. Manik, the fourth brother was Police Patel in an adjacent village (Robinson 1988: 68, 72). It will shortly be sketched how they[55] controlled their fellow villagers in the seventies.

An important element of the power exercised by the family over other villagers, like elsewhere in India, was the use or threat of physical force. Only the Patels were considered to have the right to beat (or order the beating of) other adult men (Robinson 1988: 42). To safeguard their power, (also, as elsewhere in India), the Reddys used the Harijans (Untouchables) as their allies. In the early 1970s,

> 'the Harijans of Mallannapalle received from the Reddy brothers employment, loans and assistance in acquiring land. In return, they provided the force required both to deliver the Mallannapalle vote bank and to attack and harass their master's political enemies. ... The Harijans insured the obedience of the Mallannapalle voters through

---

[53] Since the states had some leeway in implementing the general design of Panchayati Raj, the powers held by officials and politicians of the different layers vary from state to state.

[54] The Police Patel Srinivas lost powerful allies in the fifties and was then boycotted, so that no villager was allowed to work on his lands. Although he retained his office, he had little influence in the village thereafter and his economic status declined (Robinson 1988: 69).

[55] As Pratap (and later Manik) repeatedly fell out with his brothers and was boycotted, it was the second brother, Lakshma and his ally Narsimha, the Headman, who were most influential.

their roles as loan collectors and labour supervisors, and by administering beatings which could both hurt and pollute' (Robinson 1988: 45).

Backed up by the threat of physical force, the brothers controlled the villagers 'by their virtual monopoly of the ability to give, or withhold, jobs and loans' (Robinson 1988: 125). Since they owned or occupied most of the land in the village, peasants had to turn to them for work[56] and consumption loans. Villagers who tried to work in other places, were beaten, their lands were occupied or their crop harvested and taken away. The brothers lent money at high (and arbitrarily changing) interest rates and thus kept their labourers in bondage. With a semblance of economic transactions, the brothers virtually acted as they wanted (Robinson 1988: 76-126).

'The control of the poorer people of Mallannapalle by these three brothers was close to absolute during the years 1970-2. The poor traded obedience for subsistence. Loss of work and loans, combined with beatings and fines acted as effective deterrents to 'unacceptable' behaviour' (Robinson 1988: 125).

A villager in Uttar Pradesh[57] summed up the peasants' situation accurately:

'[The landlords] are afraid that if there is enough food in our stomachs, we will no longer work for them. They keep us in debt by cheating us and charging high interest rates which we never can return. They treat us like shoes and abuse our women. They beat us if we work elsewhere or come late to them. They are so big, they can do as they like. How can we dare to oppose them? Then we cannot even go out of our houses, for all the land around is owned by them' (Sharma 1968: 170, after Robinson 1988: 116).

The propertied group was controlled by additional measures. The merchants were forced to give large loans to the Reddys (especially at the time of elections) and if they were disobedient, their money was not repaid. Reddy rivals were often boycotted, which meant that no one was allowed to work or interact with them. 'Underlying the success of these techniques was, again the threat of force ... for the higher castes, the threat of being beaten by a Harijan was a powerful sanction' (Robinson 1988: 134).

Obedience to the Reddys included voting as ordered in elections. Robinson (1988: 169) estimated that Lakshma and Narsimha controlled between 1,000

---

[56] The brothers also ran toddy shops, a sugarcane factory and a rice mill and bought and sold cattle (forcibly, at more than double the usual price) to the villagers (Robsinson 1988: 133).
[57] This is a good summary of the same situation elsewhere in India.

and 2,000 votes[58]. The same system of controls and vote-delivery was perpetuated upwards:

> 'Narsapur politics, while dominated by the landowners, was financed largely by the resources of the Komatis [Merchants] and facilitated by the threat of (polluting) force provided by the Harijans. ... The village leaders (landowners) borrowed from the Komatis and lent to the taluk political leaders (large landowners). In utilizing these loans the candidate was not only able to secure funds but also the support of the village leader's vote bank, and of the Komatis from whom the village leaders borrowed (which also yielded the votes of those whom the Komatis were able to influence, particularly their debtors – Robinson 1988: 177).

The system worked in Narsapur for two decades. 'By the mid-1970s, however, national economic and political strategies began to have critical, and often unexpected effects on local political processes' (Robinson 1988: 187). The central government passed new land ceiling laws, under which some of the brother's land was declared surplus in 1972. However, in 1981 the land had still not been taken by the government and no other land had been redistributed to villagers either. While the law had almost no immediate practical impact, there was another consequence: Since superior government officials and the Communist leader V. Reddy made an effort to publicise the ceiling laws, villagers thought that the Reddys could possibly lose some of their land. Lakshma and Narsimha cultivated the same fear and ceased giving loans. As Lakshma commented:

> 'Why would I give loans if I cannot take their lands on mortgage? It is useless to give loans if you have to depend on the mercy of your debtor in order to recover the loan' (Robinson 1988: 189-90).

Between 1973 and 1975, the brothers got into financial difficulties. After retreating from the lucrative moneylending business, they had to confront management problems at the factory and the toddy shops. The central government put new emphasis on the prosecution of tax evaders and passed legislation to free small peasants from their ever-increasing debts to moneylenders. Unlike before, bureaucrats (whose power was significantly increased during the Emergency because of the supsension of the powers of local

---

[58] Unitl 1971, ballot boxes were opened at the polling stations and control of how the village votes were cast was possible. From 1971 to 1981, the ballots were jointly counted at the constituency headquarters, but most people continued to vote as ordered because they feared that the Reddys could find out (Robinson 1988: 151-2). After 1981, the votes were again counted locally, which reinstated the village leader's control (Robinson 1988: 242).

political bodies) refused to be bribed by the Reddy brothers and started to implement the laws. As a local government official commented in 1977:

> 'We knew about their (the Reddy brother's) illegal and tyrannical activities and we were determined to break their power. We wanted to show the people of these villages that they could live as human beings' (Robinson 1988: 196).

Lakshma, the dominant brother, who had 'developed his financial interests on the twin assumption that officials could be bribed and that labour would obey', was caught by surprise (Robinson 1988: 196). In 1975, local officials, including the Subcollector, the Tehsildar and police and tax officials pressed Lakshma for payment of all outstanding taxes. At the same time, they told the villagers not to repay their loans, which had become illegal under the new law. Lakshma's enemies were eager to support the officials, among them a local Communist leader, a political opponent from an adjacent village, one of Lakshma's business partners, Kishan, and his brothers Manik and Pratap, who had formed an alliance against him and Narsimha. Kishan even paid Manik to encourage the villagers to oppose Lakshma. Those who refused to repay their loans to Lakshma got money from Manik as a bonus. It was not difficult to convince the villagers. As one merchant from a neighbouring village said: 'Everyone had some reason to oppose Lakshma' (Robinson 1988: 197-8).

In June 1975, Lakshma received several notices demanding his payment of the excise tax. As he did not react, the Tehsildar, tax officials and reserve police came to the village and auctioned stored paddy belonging to him. Lakshma and Narsimha ordered their attached labourers and Harijans to burn the government lorry. A fight broke out, and the brothers fled. When the police came to enquire who had been responsible for the incident, Pratap and Manik named thirty-four supporters of Lakshma, most of which had not actually been involved. All were arrested and Lakshma and Narsimha later also surrendered on the advice of their lawyer (Robinson 1988: 201). As their case could be called any time, all of them had to stay in Sangareddy to be available on short notice. Lakshma rented a house for them to stay in. Madiga Bhoomiah, the Harijan who collected loans for the Reddy brothers, reported what happened in that house:

> 'We had a lot of time with nothing to do, so we talked. We found we were all against Lakshma and Narsimha. We were always losing' (Robinson 1988: 202).

Lakshma and Narsimha were sentenced to three years of jail, while the others were reprimanded. It took another two years until their appeal was decided (Robinson 1988: 202).

Six months later, Narsimha lost the post of Village Headman on a no confidence vote[59] (Robinson 1988: 202). Four reasons were stated:

> '(1) The Gram Panchayat is supposed to meet at least twice a year, but, except for elections, no meeting had been held during the seventeen years Narsimha had been Sarpanch: False reports had been sent to the Panchayat Samiti office stating that such meetings had been held. (2) Neither the Sarpanch nor the Upa Sarpanch had done anything to benefit the villages of this Gram Panchayat, and had neither informed the people about, nor helped them to make use of, government loans and other facilities. (3) They had not visited the villages to see what the problems of the people were. Or, as one man put it 'They do not need to see our problems; they are our problem.' (4) 'The Sarpanch has eaten the money from a road contract, but where is the road?"' (Robinson 1988: 203).

All Panches were given police protection on the day of the meeting. The Subcollector conducted the vote. Two months later, new elections were held. Narsimha and Gollapur Ram, an uneducated worker, but an elder of the 'respectable' Munnur cultivator caste, contested. The vote was split 6-3. Narsimha and his enemy Kishan, who backed Ram, made payments to Panches to 'change their opinion' (Robinson 1988: 204). The vote was by secret ballot and Gollapur Ram won by 5-4 (Robinson 1988: 205).

Now Narsimha also began to lose the support of the Harijans. The loan collector Madiga Bhoomiah, who was no longer needed, commented:

> 'When I was taken to court because of the lorry burning, I realized what was happening. All those Patels are trying to exploit the Harijans and other service castes. Now I have stopped collecting loans. I owe Lakshma nothing. I no longer work for him and I am doing my own cultivation.'

Mala Peddiah, the Harijan labour foremen continued to work for Narsimha, but privately agreed with Bhoomaiah, saying:

> 'The Patels have helped us to get loans from the government for cattle, wells, grain. Yet what happens? Most of what we get goes right back to the Patels. They are not really helping us' (Robinson 1988: 206).

When the 1977 Parliamentary Elections approached, both the Congress and the Communist candidate did not visit Narsimha and Lakshma privately as before, but held open meetings conversing directly with the villagers.

---

[59] Even though elections were forbidden under the Emergency, Mallannapalle situation was considered to be a special case (Robinson 1988: 202).

Lakshma and Narsimha did not make recommendations on how to vote as they had quarrels with the Communist candidate, but held the Congress government responsible for their troubles. Villagers commented that this were their first 'instruction-free' elections (Robinson 1988: 209). While the Janata Party won nationwide, Andhra Pradesh remained a stronghold of the Congress Party. As a consequence, all officials were transferred out of the area. The court case against Lakshma and Narsimha was dismissed and the brothers started to rebuild their power. However, as Robinson summarised:

> 'Much had changed in Mallannapalle. The events behind the lorry burning, the court case, and the government's role in the no-confidence vote, had undermined the Reddy brother's position as brokers with the outside world. Their hold on Mallannapalle debtors had decreased as a result of the government-encouraged, non-repayment tactics of the mid-1970s. The Harijan's perception that their best interests were not necessarily with the Reddys had taken root. While the former had not actively opposed the latter, they tried to avoid both working for the Reddys and participating in their disputes. Also, as Lakshma's and Narsimha's control over Pratap and Manik, and over the other Mallannapalle landowners and village elders diminished, the demand and competition for labour increased. In addition, the availability of government loans and new economic programmes had begun to provide some alternatives for both attached and daily labourers' (Robinson 1988: 211).

Pratap also lost some influence, when the powerful and lucrative posts of Police and Mali Patel were combined and given to the Police Patel (Robinson 1988: 216). 'While the Mallannapalle Reddys were vying for [new] position in the local arenas', further changes occurred, facilitated by

> 'improved communications, increased implementation of new (and old) government policies, growing competition for labour [and] the changing role of the Harijans' (Robinson 1988: 216).

A bus route was established between Narsapur and Mallannapalle (Robinson 1988: 216-7), the functioning of the school improved considerably and a government television set was installed, which became popular with the villagers,

> 'for entertainment and for information about agriculture, health, family planning and other government programmes' (Robinson 1988: 217).

The TV shows also gave the villagers a comparative perspective. One worker related this story:

> 'We saw a programme on television which showed labourers working in the Peddapalle village (in Nasarpur taluk). They were doing the same work we do, but they were earning nearly Rs 2 a day more than we were. We told the Patels that we must have the same pay. We did not get the full amount, but we got most of it.'

In the late 70s, the Agricultural Indebtedness Relief Act was widely discussed. It established that private creditors were not legally allowed to recover loans from agricultural workers who owned less than five acres of land. The debtor's resolve not to repay their loans and the Reddy's decision not to lend money out were thus strengthened. Credit from both private and government banks became slowly available (Robinson 1988: 217). Gollapur Ram was Village Headman until 1981 and spread information about government schemes to the villagers (Robinson 1988: 218). Many used government loans explicitly to avoid attachment to their employees, who 'complained continually about the difficulties of acquiring attached labourers' (Robinson 1988: 219).

The Harijans began to use the leadership skills developed under the Reddys for their own benefit (Robinson 1988: 223). The former loan collector, Bhoomaiah organised yearly labour strikes. The tractor driver said in 1980:

> 'For the past three years we had a strike each year. We told our employers that we would not continue to work unless our pay was raised. Every year we got a raise. Madiga Bhoomaiah is our leader. He is our guru; he teaches us how to act with the Patels. He is our representative when we talk with them' (Robinson 1988: 225).

During the Legislative Assembly Elections in 1978, Lakshma and Narsimha again did not campaign for a candidate, as the Harijans were unwilling to help them (Robinson 1988: 231). Villagers voted on personal preferences, 'giving a variety of reasons for voting as they did' (Robinson 1988: 232).

In summary, between 1957 and 1972, villagers depended on landowners because of their control over land and labour, the merchant's money and the Harijan's physical force. Therefore, they obeyed them and voted as demanded, so that village leaders could deliver vote banks to candidates at upper political levels. However, as the leader's control over land and labour diminished because of new laws, improved implementa-tion, increased competition for labour and new sources of credit, the Harijans and attached labourers ceased to supply force on demand. The village vote banks collapsed and villagers began to vote individually (Robinson 1988: 248).

The 1981 Panchayat elections saw new reforms in place. The provision of direct and simultaneous elections for Panch, Sarpanch and Panchayat

Samiti president minimised party interference, as intended. Vote count by block, however, 'undermined the progress made since 1971 in protecting the secrecy of the ballot. Once again fear constituted a crucial component of the voting process and certainly played a major role in Narsimha's re-election as Sarpanch of the newly constituted Mallannapalle Gram Panchayat. Still,

> 'the 1981 Panchayat elections followed the general pattern which had been developing since 1977. Mallannapalle Gram Panchayat voters had begun casting their votes for a variety of reasons. These included both fear of Lakshma and Narsimha and disapproval of their past records; caste affiliations; personal alliances or enmities with the candidates; village loyalties; and anticipated direct benefits from the government (as well as from the candidates)' (Robinson 1988: 250).

III.3.2.b. Five Indian Villages in 1999-2000

The publication 'Seeing the State. Governance and Governmentality in India', published in 2005 by Stuart Corbridge et al. draws on two research projects carried out in five villages in rural eastern India between 1999 and 2001. Seven field assistants lived in the villages from March 1999 to March 2000 and information was collected primarily by an extensive questionnaire survey, in which five hundred (mostly poor) households participated (Corbridge et al. 2005: 10-1). There were 250 to 300 households in each locality. The research started with a household census. Thereafter, group interviews were conducted and the researchers collected information from 100 randomly sampled households in each locality, 80 of which were poor according to the researcher's definition[60] (Corbridge et al. 2005: 88-9). Additionally, 280 taped interviews were conducted with teachers, Block Development Officers (BDOs), District Development Officers, engineers, trade unionists, contractors, politicians, brokers and other informants at the Block, District and State levels (Corbridge et al. 2005: 10-1).

The distribution of land in all the villages surveyed was highly unequal (Corbridge et al. 2005: 88) and many informants suffered from severe income poverty. Most of the poorest households belonged to the Scheduled Communities or Other Backward Classes (see footnote 9 in chapter II.2 for elaboration). As low wages[61] prevailed, unemployment in the off-seasons rapidly pushed them into distress (Corbridge et al. 2005: 93).

---

[60] Corbridge et al (2005: 93) developed their own definition of poverty. They considered a household poor when it relied only on unskilled labour for its income, did not have full employment or had a non-favourable ratio of earner to dependants.
[61] Wages were at or below the government minimum wage of Rs. 48 (US $ 1) per day.

Caste was still of importance in the villages surveyed, although this had started to be challenged in some places:

> 'In Bihar ... to be a chamar or a dusadh [Untouchables] is to be of low social worth – polluting, even – in the eyes of higher-caste villagers. These prejudices are being challenged in Bhojpur, especially, where slights to the honour of the Scheduled Castes can escalate quickly into public confrontations, but these changes are occuring in a context where caste remains ever visible as a social marker. Elsewhere, caste or ethnic divisions are not as actively politicized, but they are far from being insignificant. In West Bengal Districts ..., adivasis [Scheduled Tribes] are marginalized for not having Bengali or Hindi as their first language, or because of their religious beliefs and cultural practices' (Corbridge et al. 2005: 95).

Gender relations were highly unequal in all villages surveyed and women suffered worst from high levels of poverty (Corbridge et al. 2005: 96).

Access to work and credit remained a major concern for the poor. Investing in good relations with employers and local patrons was therefore important. Loans to poor households (belonging to Scheduled Castes or Tribes), which were most often needed for consumption in off-seasons, were mainly provided by their regular employers, who charged interest rates of five to ten per cent per month. Government loans were not sufficiently available as an alternative in any of the villages (Corbridge et al. 2005: 102-3). Corbridge et al. summarised:

> 'For the poor in each of our Districts, groups of 'local uppers' – individuals with economic and/or political resources – are important sources of support. Although the social networks these individuals produce vary greatly, a number of general points still emerge. ... the *resources controlled by employers and moneylenders are key to the survival strategies of many among the poor. Government* assistance provides access to work, credit and other benefits for some people, but it *does little to diminish the role of the economically powerful*' (Corbridge et al. 2005: 107, my italics).

Even when poorer people did approach state institutions, they were mostly assisted by middlemen, who were often political workers or richer villagers. Thus, 'staying in the right side of powerful intermediaries' was crucial (Corbridge et al. 2005: 107).

The poor generally wished to educate their sons, so that they would have the possibility of taking on new jobs outside of agriculture. They also mentioned that education would help them against being cheated.

Daughters were educated in order to have an advantage on the 'marriage and dowry markets'. However,

> 'children [were] receiving less education than would be considered desirable by their parents [which was] mainly a product of economic hardship. ... Parents also voiced concerns about the quality and utility of the education that children were receiving in government schools' (Corbridge et al. 2005: 99).

Villagers encountered the state in schools, health care centres and in the police stations, to name just a few examples, but Corbridge et al. chose to focus their study on the developmental state, as I have also done in my paper. We should not forget, however, that all the institutions together 'contribute[d] to [the villager's] senses of how, and for whom, government operate[d]' (Corbridge et al. 2005: 114).

III.3.2.c. Personalised Power in Bihar

The village studied by the research team in Bidupur Block in Bihar (Vaishali District) was situated on the northern bank of the Ganges, 40 kilometres from the city Patna and with ready access to its market. Facilitated by canal irrigation, agriculture was more capital-intensive than in other villages and many farmers grew bananas. The Block was politically dominated by the high-caste Yadavs and 99 out of the 318 households were classified as belonging to 'Other Backward Classes' (see footnote 9 in chapter II.2, Corbridge et al. 2005: 92). In 1999, sixty-nine percent of the men and thirty-five percent of the women in the District could read and write (Corbridge et al. 2005: 97).

Higher-caste leaders provided work and loans and also played an important part in mediating village disputes. The other centre of power in the village – recognised by the poor and the rich alike – was BB, the local Member of the Legislative Council, who belonged to Laloo Yadav's Rashtriya Janata Dal party and controlled most government-funded development programmes. The third person who was an important source of support for the poor was the government's Village Level Worker. If the poor wanted to access individualised state support, for instance in the form of pensions, loans or improved housing under the Indira Awas Yojana scheme, they turned to him and often had to pay for his assistance (Corbridge et al. 2005: 104-5). Formal government institutions were weak, because all Panchayats had been suspended in Bihar in 1999 (Corbridge et al. 2005: 105). Political competition in the area was however considerable and often organised along caste lines (Corbridge et al. 2005: 11).

When the research team talked to the former District Magistrate, who had long worked in Vaishali, he told them that during his long tenure, he had 'adopted a quota system wherein local politicians were asked to recommend and decide upon the schemes that would operate in their constituencies' (Corbridge et al. 2005: 174).

All funds that were approved were simply divided on a 30:70 basis between the Members of the national Parliament (MPs), and the Members of the state's Legislative Assembly (MLAs) or – as in this case – the Member of the Legislative Council, who could use the money as he deemed appropriate without any further official interference. BB had used his share to have development schemes set up in all the villages where he had influential supporters (Corbridge et al. 2005: 173) who became his executing agents. While the District Magistrate (DM) had thus 'ceded power to the MLAs in recognition of their local dominance' (Corbridge et al. 2005: 174), he still tried to ensure that funds also went to those villages that were ignored by both BB and the MLA RR, because they supported rival politicians or were simply considered irrelevant. Using money accrued to the development funds, he set up schemes in these areas. He commented:

> 'If any MLA or ruling party leaders questioned as to why I was sanctioning projects in areas of their political rivals, I would say that that was being done out of the discretionary DM's funds and did not encroach upon their quota, hence they could not have any grievances nor any locus standi to object this' (Corbridge et al. 2005: 174).

Development works were handed out to contractors, who, as we have already seen in the case study of Irrigation Management by Wade, were also 'required to function as political go-betweens' (Corbridge et al. 2005: 195). They organised the work and labourers and additionally, 'the appropriate cuts and commissions [had to] be passed on to officials and politicians with minimum fuss' (Corbridge et al. 2005: 195). Contractors in Vaishali were normally tied to politicians and required a public reputation for being 'so-and-so's man'. At election times, they were also expected to deliver votes to the MLAs and MPs they were connected to. In order to do so, they spread rumours about rival candidates, hired vehicles and equipment and organised rallies for visiting politicians, whom they also supplied with meals and hospitality. Some also engaged in acts of 'booth capture' for their political bosses (Corbridge et al. 2005: 196).

Villagers also turned to contractors for assistance when they had to approach higher-ranking bureaucrats or politicians. The contractors as well as other political agents were called 'chhoto bhai netas' locally, which means 'little brother leaders', because villagers were quite aware that real power was not in their hands, but in that of their more powerful allies. At the same time, as Corbridge et al. interpreted, this term might encapsulate both the villagers 'ambivalence towards politics, and the attempt to tame or capture it within local frames of reference' (Corbridge et al. 2005: 198).

III.3.2.d. Participation in West Bengal

The village studied in Debra Block in West Bengal was made up of three hamlets, eight kilometres from the nearest small market centre. It had a large population of Santal and Bhumji people, who were listed as a Scheduled Tribe by the government. The whole area had benefitted from micro-irrigaton and the recent growth of flower cultivation for the Kolkata market (Corbridge et al. 2005: 91-2). Literacy rates were high, eighty-one percent of the men and fifty-four percent of the women could read and write, which was in large part due to the Total Literacy Campaign which had been active in the area in the 1990s (Corbridge et al. 2005: 97).

Marvin Davis had presented politics in the area in the 1970s as a contest between rival village elites, but, thirty years later, 'these days ha[d] largely passed' (Davis 1983, after Corbridge et al. 2005: 195). Since then, the Communist party in the area had mobilised groups within the rural poor (Corbridge et al. 2005: 11). The state's Left Front Government had also made an effort to raise levels of participation and in this village, at least, it had been successful (Corbridge et al. 2005: 117). Panchayat members and party workers dominated many areas of public life. Six male activists of the Communist party (CPI-M, M for Marxist) and its female council member lived in the village and 'were active in helping households in all manner of tasks, from school registration to settling wage disputes' (Corbridge et al. 2005: 106). Three of them fell below the poverty line designated by the researchers and only two were caste Hindus. Thus, it was accurate to say that their 'social and economic backgrounds reflected those of their constituents' (Corbridge et al. 2005: 106). In interviews, villagers said that they trusted the party members. As one informant said about a party worker: 'He is the friend of the poor, knowledgeable and a good person. All people respect him' (Corbridge et al. 2005: 106). It was considered valuable that the party members both knew how to handle the government and also knew about the situation of the poor. As another informant put it: 'He is my neighbour. He knows my condition' (Corbridge et al. 2005: 106). Many villagers reported that they turned to the female member of the Gram Panchayat if a dispute needed to be settled. In spite of her gender, caste and economic poverty, she held a powerful position in the village by virtue of her office. As opposition members also resided within the village, there were many contact points between villagers and branches of the state. Low-level government officers often visited the village, but other civil servants had to be contacted through Panchayat members. Corbridge et al. summarised that '[p]anchayat representatives [from diverse social backgrounds] had thus displaced the leadership roles played by larger landlords before the 1970s' (Corbridge et al. 2005: 106).

In May 1999, members of the research team observed a statutory village meeting. These 'Gram Sansad' meetings were conducted twice a year in every ward. It was chaired by the ward's Gram Panchayat member who was assisted by the Panchayat Secretary. Representatives of the Block-level Panchayat and government officers also attended the meeting. The proceedings were formal and business-like. The Block Panchayat member reported on general progress in village development and gave exact figures about how much money had been assigned to the Panchayat under various government schemes. He also reported on the Gram Panchayat's efforts to raise money through afforestation schemes and a toll tax and asked the villagers to be more health conscious and make use of the sanitary scheme. After this introduction, development priorities were discussed. The elected representatives and party members did not actively take part in the discussions, because – as the researchers later found out – they had primed villagers to make suggestions on their behalf (Corbridge et al. 2005: 117-8). However,

> 'the discussion we observed still managed to break away from a scripted performance. Figures for government spending were contested and the failings of Panchayat members were pointed out. Alternative plans were also proposed, particularly by wealthier, educated villagers, and members of the opposition parties. These and other 'disruptions' were handled in a professional manner by the elected members who chaired the meeting' (Corbridge et al. 2005: 118).

III.3.3. Politics & Corruption: Findings

In this chapter, I will summarise the findings generated from the case studies presented above and draw on further literature to arrive at an understanding of the connections between politics and corruption, which takes into account the complexity of local situations.

The first chapters focus on what strategies local leaders employ to sustain their power (III.3.3.a) and in how far they cooperate with or compete against each other (III.3.3.b). In their contest for political power, most actors publicly condemn venality and often accuse opponents of being corrupt, especially during election campaigns. Because the media reports on these accusations and also investigates cases of fraud on its own, corruption is today a frequently depated topic in many regions, suggests the next chapter (III.3.3.c, compare also chapter I.2.2).

Whether this encourages citizens to demand more accountability depends on local circumstances. The following section (III.3.3.d) looks at settings in which politics are clientelistic and controlled by a few political actors and their intermediaries, who are investigated in detail in section III.3.3.e. Thereafter, I will look at settings in which power is less personalised and villagers participate more actively in political decision-making (III.3.3.f). As the last point, the topic of villager's mobilisation and politicisation will be further elaborated (III.3.3.g). As always, the final paragraph III.3.3.h attempts to sketch how politicial players make sense of corruption.

III.3.3.a. Economic Power & Force

'[I]n India, democracy was constructed against the grain, both of a society founded upon the inequality of the caste order, and of an imperial and authoritarian state' (Khilnani 2004: 9).

In the first case study presented above, the Reddy brother's near-total control over villagers depended primarily on their economic power. As a result, they also controlled physical force and bureaucratic and political posts within the village and nobody dared to oppose them. Their position of power began to decline when their arbitrary rule over the village was challenged by bureaucrats – who had been given new instructions and a wider range of power during the Emergency.

Robinson argued that since Independence, 'poverty in India [was] an essential component of the power structure, the reverse [was] equally true', because rural elites had at the same time assured that 'the poor remain[ed] a source of cheap, available, and docile labour' and also controlled 'the votes, and thereby the point of articulation between the villagers and the higher levels of government' (Robinson 1988: 8). She complained that a lot of the literature on local level politics missed this point. As she summarised:

'Far from interpreting the needs of the people, providing them guidance or effecting their modernization, the local elites have often used their knowledge of the 'local idiom' to depress the poor further, thereby increasing their tentacular control over access to the lower strata of the Indian bureaucracy...
As the Mallannapalle Village Council Headmen (Sarpanch) put it, 'People will not obey if they are given too much food. If you put too much oil in your engine it will not start. People are the same" (Robinson 1988: 9).

In the introduction to the following, more recent, case studies, we could see that even though the rural elite's monopoly may have been weakened, it still remained important for poorer villagers, to stay on the right side of local uppers who could provide employment and were the major source of credit, as government loans were still not sufficiently available. Corbridge et al. (2005: 107) summarised that

> '*Government* assistance provides access to work, credit and other benefits for some people, but it *does little to diminish the role of the economically powerful.*'

However, this is certainly not equally true for both the villages presented. The differences are informative and will be discussed more under III.3.3.g.

III.3.3.b. Elite Competition & Accommodation

Even if government schemes were not sufficiently financed to curb the power of local grandees, they were an important source of patronage and controlling them could also lead to a sizeable illicit earning as Wade's case study (II.2.2.c) showed. Competition for access to public posts and benefits was therefore immense and fought for on many different planes.

Khilnani also linked questions of identity to this quest:

> 'After fifty years of an Indian state, the definition of who is an Indian is as passionately contested as ever. What keeps it in contest is the presence of the state whose access to resources makes it a real prize, and the persistence of democratic politics, which has kept most people in the game for this prize. The contest is over economic opportunities and about cultural recognition: it is a contest for ownership of the state. The intensity of that conflict can be seen in the dizzying assortment of claims upon that state, claims that have been at once agitated and frustrated by democracy and economic progress' (Khilnani 2004: 195).

As Corbridge et al. underlined, caste still mattered greatly in Bihar, but, in accordance with Khilnani's argument, 'more in terms of a person's ability to mobilize resources for a named group than in terms of abstract ideas about moral hierarchy' (Corbridge et al. 2005: 198). Development programmes provided key resources for actors in the political society and one 'should reiterate that the involvement of 'politicians' in the operation of these programmes [was] not wholly parasitic. It [was] to some degree a valid expression of their social power' (Corbridge et al. 2005: 199).

Corbridge's research team witnessed active political societies in the areas of research. These included 'political parties and their operatives, local political brokers and councillors, and perhaps even lower-level public servants who depend upon the grace and favour of politicians', all of which - 'bridged between the government and the public' (Corbridge et al. 2005: 189). They argued that these players drew their strengths 'from the ability to exercise control over events in the locality and link these to wider political discourses that emanate[d] from Kolkata, Patna, Delhi and elsewhere' (Corbridge et al. 2005: 190), a subject taken up in chapter III.3.3.c.

These players collaborated or competed, depending on local power configurations. Paul Brass argued that in North India, like in Mallannapalle of the seventies, it was the local elite which exercised control 'over a corrupt police force and an increasingly demoralized bureaucracy' (after Corbridge & Harris 2000: 201). As the discussion of Good Governance suggests (compare chapter III.2.3.d), this was also because government offices were often underfinanced and understaffed, and could therefore, for instance, not always protect citizens from acts of violence or prevent 'booth capture' everywhere. Khilnani summarised that the Indian state was

> 'far from supremely effective: it regularly fail[ed] to protect its citizens against physical violence, it [did] not provide them with welfare, and it ha[d] not fulfilled its extensive ambitions to transform Indian society' (Khilnani 2004: 59).

That is why, as Corbridge and Harris argued, following Brass,

> 'in ... Bihar or Uttar Pradesh the lack of accountability of government at the local level ha[d] encouraged subaltern social movements to challenge the authority of the state from without. Naxalism [see footnote 24 in Chapter III.2.] is often mentioned in this regard, and the Chipko andolan [social movement] has been widely acclaimed for its anti-state and anti-development outlook' (Corbridge and Harris 2000: 201).

However, as Gupta pointed out and as Robinson's study showed, government interference in local matters on the side of the poor, though infrequent and imperfect – often wholly rhetorically – had given them heightened self-esteem and began to irritate local elites. New laws (Robinson 1988: 189-90) and public discussions on accountability (Gupta 1995, compare chapter III.1.2.g) further encouraged them, cautiously, but persistently, to challenge political domination, knowing that they would have to protect themselves against retaliation from the uppers.

Corbridge and Harris (2000: 206) argued, that while empowerment of subaltern groups was mostly achieved against the state, 'citizens movements [were] most successful where they ... forced the state apparatus to become responsive to their interest'.[62]

---

[62] In another village studied by Corbridge et al (2005) in Sahar Block, Bhojpur District

In our first case study of Mallannapalle village, politics and bureaucrats were closely intertwined. Indeed, in that case it would be ironic to suggest that bureaucrats could be disinterested professionals (as Gupta had pointed out, compare chapter I.3). Instead, Village Officers, lower-level bureaucrats, were drawn from the local elite and competed with politicians for power. Depending on the situation, bureaucrats can be controlled by politicians or vice versa, or both can be controlled by local patrons. In Mallannapalle of the 1970s, it was Narsimha, the brother who did not hold any office, who controlled the locality. But bureaucrats, especially higher-ranking ones, held an alternate, though varying, degree of power by virtue of their office.

Bureaucrats lacked sufficient resources to compete against local patrons, but sometimes they could make use of an opening and carve out spaces of power for themselves. However, whether this enhanced accountability towards the people or simply led to a corrupt nexus between them and the politicians, depended on local levels of political mobilisation and leadership, as we will see in chapter III.3.g.

In the next, more recent case studies, while local patrons were still strong, there were also alternate powerholders (the Village Level Workers, MLAs and superior bureaucrats) which citizens could petition– mostly with the aid of a bribe – and even the most powerful politicians in the area were careful to assign development schemes to the villages which supported them in the elections. What Robinson had said about her South Indian village in the 1980s, continued to be true in other parts of India and might represent a general trend:

> 'It became evident during both the 1981 Panchayat elections, and the 1983 assembly elections that the links between votes and development were now explicit, clearly discernible, and widely understood' (Robinson 1988: 236).

As Ruud (Ruud 2001: 134, after Corbridge et al. 2005: 190) pointed out, ordinary Indians were quite prepared to acknowledge that politics had to be based on 'compromises, alliances (sometimes with old enemies), deals and

---

in Bihar, a Naxalite group (the CPI-ML) had fought against the local elite (organised as the Ranveer Sena – Corbridge et al 2005: 11, 105). The violence had recently quietened down, the CPI-ML had entered into political competition and public hearings ('Janata Durbars') were conducted regularly and attended by higher-level bureaucrats to sort out conflicts before they escalated into violence. These Janata Durbars 'had the effect of making higher-level government officers much more visible here than in the other Districts: villagers were more aware of the presence of these officers, and were sometimes able to petition them directly for different forms of government support' (Corbridge et al 2005: 105).

power equations' and were often 'dirty'. Therefore, they tended to judge politicians by 'their ability and capacity to get things done' (Ruud 2001: 130, after Corbridge et al. 2005: 190). It was less important to them how much politicians 'skimmed off' development funds, what mattered was how much reached them in the end (compare also chapter III.2.2.b). This 'helps to explain why corruption and violence are often part of the political process, no matter how much they are sniffed at in the literatures on civil society' (Corbridge et al. 2005: 190).

III.3.3.c. Political Rhetoric & the Media

What we have seen in all the case studies of political corruption was 'the playing out of power relations between government officials, local power holders and the poor'. This 'power-play ha[d] important implications for the state's reproduction, both as a system and as an idea', as Corbridge et al. rightly pointed out. They summarised that

> '[e]ncounters with the developmental state also build up a dynamic picture of 'it', both as an idealized set of values and practices (the state as it should work), and also as its flawed but more commonly experienced counterpart (the state as it does work)' (Corbridge et al. 2005: 120).

In the struggle for control of the resources controlled by the state, the discourse about corruption can become a potent weapon. As Gupta analysed about the region in Western Uttar Pradesh, where he did research:

> 'The landowning caste in this region ha[d] become fairly prosperous as they [were] the chief beneficiaries of the Green Revolution. But this newfound wealth ha[d] yet to be translated into bureaucratic power and cultural capital. In other words, given the central role that state institutions play[ed] in rural life, these groups [sought] to stabilize the conditions for the reproduction of their dominance. Because they perceive[d] the state to be acting against their interests, they deploy[ed] the discourse of corruption to undermine the credibility of the state and to attack the manner in which the government organizations operate[d]' (Gupta 1995: 389).

The politicians interviewed by Pavarala, though asserting their own integrity, also frequently accused political rivals of corruption (Pavarala 1996: 228). Corbridge et al. witnessed that politicians in the five villages surveyed drew 'tactically on a range of ideas about moral duty to justify their behaviour' towards the villagers (Corbridge et al. 2005: 197).

As mentioned earlier, where Gupta and Parry did research, corruption was indeed a topic that was hotly debated (compare chapter III.1.2.g), because politicians accused their opponents of being corrupt, openly and through spreading rumours (contractors were supposed to spread rumours as a service to their political patrons in Bidupur Block, Bihar – compare chapter III.3.2.c). While Gupta emphasised that rumours were

> 'an especially effective vehicle to challenge official accounts, especially when agencies of the state transgress[ed] local standards of behaviour' (Gupta 1995: 388),

he also focused on the role of the media in the discursive construction of the state and in setting and reifying standards of accountability.

During his fieldwork in 1984-5 and 1989, he analysed local editions of six Hindi newspapers[63] in the Mandi area, which widely circulated among villagers. He found that they pursued stories of corruption with greater zeal than their metropolitan counterparts. They also made a practice of naming specific departments and officials within the state bureaucracy and thus

> 'maintained a richer sense of the multilayered nature of the state because their reportage was necessarily focused on events in different localities, which corresponded to lower levels of the state hierarchy' (Gupta 1995: 387).

In most of the stories, higher-level officials were depicted as being unresponsive to complaints and it was often suggested that they were complicit with corrupt practices of lower-ranking officers, as Wade had also showed (compare chapter III.2.2.c).

Another interesting finding was that newspapers put a special emphasis on the construction of the public.

> 'A common discursive practice was to talk of 'the public' (janata) that was being openly exploited by the police, or 'the citizens' (naagarik) who were harassed by blackmarketeering or 'the people' (log) whose clear accusation against the hospital was given voice in the paper, or 'simple farmers' (bholaay-bhaalaay kisaan) who were ruthlessly exploited by the land consolidation officer' (Gupta 1995: 387).

He analysed that

> 'these reports ... created subjects who were being represented as being exploited, powerless and outraged. I foreground the newspapers' functions in order to draw attention to the rhetorical strategy deployed by the mass media to galvanize into action citizens who expect state institutions to be accountable to them' (Gupta 1995: 388).

---

[63] Aaj, Dainik Jaagran, Amar Ujaala, Hindustan, Rashtriya Sahaara, and Jansatta.

While the media gave detailed attention to the performance of the local state, it also reported regional, national and international events and provided a connection between local and translocal discourses. As Gupta summarised in his article,

> 'any analysis of the state requires us to conceptualize a space that is constituted by the intersection of local, regional, national, and transnational phenomena. Accordingly, I have stressed the role of public culture in the discursive construction of the state. Bringing the analysis of public culture together with the everyday practices of lower levels of the bureaucracy helps us understand how the reality of translocal entities comes to be felt by villagers and officials' (Gupta 2005: 392).

However, he cautioned his readers that the 'discourse of accountability' created in the newspapers, politician's speeches and accusations of each other, rumours and everyday discussions among villagers, would not automatically become politically significant. Whether it did or not, depended on local circumstances and the 'level of organization of different groups that [were] affected by it' (Gupta 1995: 397).

III.3.3.d. Personalised Power

In the villages investigated by Corbridge et al., different forms of political organisation and levels of political mobilisation existed. Here and in chapter III.3.3.f, I want to have a look at the two 'extremes'. To do so, I will briefly introduce one more case study. As in Bidupur Block in Bihar (compare chapter III.3.2.c), power in the village studied in Murhu Block, Ranchi District in what is now the Indian state of Jharkhand, was personalised to a large degree. The village was primarily inhabited by indigenous Adivasis and despite the suspension of the power of the Panchayats[64], the former village Headman, called Mukhiya regionally, 'still acted as virtually the sole conduit to the government development bureaucracy'. Within the local office, the Mukhiya had the reputation of being 'developmentally minded' and was assigned several projects for his village, the benefits of which had been broadly distributed to different social groups (Corbridge et al. 2005: 106). Villagers generally applauded him 'for his ability to access a series of government schemes 'for the betterment of the village" (Corbridge et al. 2005: 197). Several villagers 'conflate[d] the position of the Mukhiya with sarkar [the state] more generally' (Corbridge et al. 2005: 115). Some thought that houses built under the Indira Awas housing scheme had actually been provided by the Mukhiya himself.

---

[64] At the time of field work, the region belonged to Bihar, where the power of the Panchayats had been suspended.

However, not everyone was content with the situation. Two unemployed young men started to challenge the position of the Mukhiya. One of them, Sudhir M, an educated young man, talked to a superior official visiting the village in order to press for the construction of a girl's toilet in the village school. With his encouragement, he went to the Block staff, who were however unwilling to pass schemes to anyone but the Mukhiya (Corbridge et al. 2005: 115). Like in Bidupur Block in Bihar, the local leader had succesfully monopolised access to government resources and used them as a source of personal patronage (Corbridge et al. 2005: 120).

However, Sudhir did not give in, and after threatening to report the reluctant bureaucrats to their superior – who had already given his approval – they conceded. He also helped some villagers to submit pension applications to the Circle Officer, who was his college friend. Thus, Sudhir started to become a local political broker in his own right.

The situation proved to be more difficult for Ranjit M, another unemployed tribal young man, who was neither as well educated nor as well connected as Sudhir. He visited the Block Office repeatedly for over a year to question the Mukhiya's dominance. The bureaucrats discouraged him:

> 'You can wear your sandals out coming here, but you won't get a scheme' (Corbridge et al. 2005: 115).

But Ranjit persisted. After talking to a Block-level Congress party worker, he found out that village open meetings were supposed to be held in order to select executing agents for development schemes, something that had never been done before in his village. The Mukhiya and Block officers had simply made up records.

> 'Armed with this information, Ranjit pushed for a proper meeting, and was successfully elected as the executing agent of the next development project in the village' (Corbridge et al. 2005: 115).

Although most villagers did not participate actively in decision-making, the Mukhiya in Murhu, as BB in Bidupur (compare chapter III.3.2.c), provided

> 'at least one model of 'Good Governance' for their supporters and even for their localities' (Corbridge et al. 2005: 175-6):

For example, the outcomes of the Employment Assurance Scheme – one of the government's development programmes whose execution Corbridge et al. examined in detail – in Murhu and Bidupur were more visible than in Midnapore. There, participation by the villagers was much better, but closer adherence to the guidelines had led to the pursuit of more labour-intensive schemes, which were of less material benefit to the locality (Corbridge et al.

2005: 175-6). Like the Mukhiya, even poorer villagers tended to prefer visible development successes rather than employment for a very limited amount of time, as Corbridge et al. reported:

> 'It is true that EAS work[ed] poorly in Bidupur from the point of view of providing employment to local people. ... Most distressing ... was the fact that the roads being built in Bidupur were mainly intended to benefit the Yadav communities and the inhabitants of what might be called the 'main villages' in the Block. ... And yet, importantly, tangible assets were built in Bidupur and a good deal of employment was provided to labouring households outside the formal structures of the EAS. Most of all, perhaps, this outcome was considered a reasonable one by most of the parties that were active in Bidupur's political society' (Corbridge et al. 2005: 174).

Furthermore, both the Mukhiya and BB (compare chapter III.3.2.c), closely worked with officials in their regions to prevent class violence in their areas, which was virulent in other parts of Bihar. They had thus

> 'provided leadership in a context in which 'the official state' [was] more fragile than it is assumed to be in the mainstream literatures on good governance. They did so, moreover, not so much by playing the part of elected local delegates, as by playing the role of the provider, or the traditional patron or dada (elder brother or bossman) figure who gets things done' (Corbridge et al. 2005: 175-6).

Through their encounters with higher-ranking officials or politicians, both Ranjit and Sudhir managed to get development schemes by using their knowledge of due process, thus challenging the Mukhiya's monopoly. Corbridge et al. commented:

> 'For some among the poor with drive and insight, chance meetings with powerful outsiders can be a first step in targeting the state' (Corbridge et al. 2005: 116).

However, their aim was neither to raise levels of political participation in the village generally nor did they act out of altruism. The style of executing power in the area (through patronage) was not altered – besides demonstrating to the villagers that the Mukhiya's power was limited – it was only that new brokers entered the competition for the allocation of schemes. Sudhir was paid 50 Rupees by each of the families which he helped to get pension applications processed and both men expected to be able to earn illicit side-incomes from the management of the schemes. Given the limited means of their families, this was a reasonable hope, judged Crobridge et al. (2005: 116).

III.3.3.e. Brokers & Contractors

As already mentioned (in the discussion of Irrigation Management in chapter III.2.2.c), since especially higher-ranking bureaucrats and politicians were reluctant of negotiating over bribes themselves, they often made use of agents or middlemen. Likewise, villagers who were unsure how to apply for government assistance, or needed help in getting it granted, or wanted to obtain an illicit benefit such as canal irrigation in an out-of-zone area, turned to local political brokers, some of which were the Mukhiya, Ranjit and Sudhir mentioned in the previous chapter.

Middlemen were either employed by officials (like the contractors in Irrigation Management and in Bidupur Block in Bihar) or known to them, for example by being a relative or friend (as in the case of Sudhir), or had acquired useful knowledge about formal procedures (like Ranjit).

The nexus between politicians and businessmen probably demands further attention, but unfortunately, there are no case studies available which look into the relationship more in detail. However, as evident in the case study of Mallannapalle, economic and political power were often closely connected. One of Parry's informants who had worked both in the public and in the private sector said that corruption levels were similarly high in both areas (Parry 2000: 53).

In his study 'Access to Development. A Study of Anti-poverty Policy and Popular Participation in two Squatter Settlements in Pune, India', where he did field research from October 1994 to May 1996 and again for two months in the winter of 1998 (van Kampen 2000: 19), Marcel van Kampen concluded that the poor were 'dependent on mediators who ha[d] better access to information and the 'means of development'', because 'the rules for participation in formal anti-poverty programmes were complicated and the application procedures [were] too bureaucratic, which [put] the poor in a disadvantaged position' (van Kampen 2000: 131-3). Within the two settlements that van Kampen studied, the brokers were local leaders and members of elite families, who justified 'their exercise of power and mediation with a façade of party politics and a relatedness to well-known political parties' (van Kampen 2000: 131-3). He judged that most of them, with only a few exceptions, were exploitative and motivated by personal interest only:

> 'Each of the two settlements [was] divided and ruled (read dominated or exploited) by two or three opposing elite families. ... I really doubt whether it matter[ed] at all which party they join[ed] with, as long as it provide[d] them local legitimisation, and protection and support from powerful external forces... Most leaders and people with leadership

ambitions in the two settlements combine[d] two motives: financial and socio-political gain, which [went] hand in hand, through the exploitation of their role as middlemen' (van Kampen 2000: 133).

Corbridge and Harris, likewise, reported for Bihar – where they did research – that poorer citizens needed intermediaries in their interactions with the bureaucracy:

'As a trip to any Block Office in Bihar will confirm, poorer men and women - and especially women - will be kept waiting for hours or even days to gain access to a government officer responsible for the allocation of pensions or some other benefit. And ... almost always with the help of a dalal (broker or contractor)' (Corbridge & Harris 2000: 202).

Parry looked at the role of middlemen in a somewhat different situation. He did participant research among 'working- and lower-middle-class people' in the large new industrial town which had sprung up around the public sector Bhilai Steel Plant in the Chattisgarh region of Madhya Pradesh for a total of sixteen months between September 1993 and April 1999 (Parry 2000: 29, 53). Adhikari, one of Parry's informants, tried to get a job in the public plant in order to maintain the family's living standard after his father's retirement ('to preserve what little they had' – Parry 2000: 41-3) and to pay for the appropriate marriages off his sisters in the 'status-preoccupied world' of his Catholic congregation (Parry 2000: 41-3). Of course, jobs in the public plant were much sought after, among other reasons, because they were for life, work was not very hard nor very long (especially when compared with the poorly paid, 'back-braking' jobs in the informal sector – Parry 2000: 36) and one could earn illicit side-incomes, for example by selling some of the cement for the plant on the black market (Parry 2000: 31). Like a multitude of other applicants, Parry's informant was prepared and willing to pay a substantial sum of money in order to have the chance to get a job in the plant, he took 'it as axiomatic' that it would cost him a minimum of Rs 40,000 – 60,000 to get a post like the one in which his father legally earned Rs. 5,000 a month (Parry 2000: 41-2). Various brokers exploited the situation by promising young men to advance their application in the official queue[65] and to use their influence over persons working in the plant to give them an advantage. Even though many of those who already worked in the plant told Parry – without prompting, and although they were not shy to admit other illegal activities – that to their own surprise they had not bribed in order to get the job (Parry 2000: 39), applicants commonly believed that payment was necessary (Parry 2000: 37). Parry sketched how intermediaries

---

[65] The official queue was so long, that by the end of 1997, applicants which had applied in 1984 were still being interviewed (Parry 2000: 37).

could exploit and sustain this impression without actually doing much. Even if it was true – in spite of the rather formal selection procedures – that members of the board had a quota of posts to fill according to their wishes, they would need agents to approach applicants and in order to protect themselves. If, for example, one member had five posts to fill and put out the word through five brokers, and these would, say, exaggerate the number of posts by a mere 20 percent, assurance could have been given to thirty candidates (Parry 2000: 38). Thus,

> 'by a kind of optical illusion, even a relatively small minority of corrupt appointments may appear to the pool of job-seekers as a rather significant majority. And 'optical illusion' is what I suspect that it quite largely is. While the world over people who have failed to get selected are predisposed to claim that something in the procedure smelt, the striking thing here is that it is not merely their mothers who believe them' (Parry 2000: 33).

While it was said that earlier, mediators would help their kinsmen without charging money, the times were supposed to be such that kinship did not count for much anymore and that brokers had to be paid. The etiquette, however, still required for both parties to pretend that the middleman was simply doing the applicant a favour by passing on his money upwards to the proper person in the plant. Parry related

> 'every second household with a son of the appropriate age in the industrial neighbourhoods in which I worked, ha[d] a story about how they paid this or that middleman a substantial sum to fix up their son in [the plant]. Of course the almost inevitable sequel [was] that there was no job and the money was never returned, or at best was only eventu-ally repaid in dribs and drabs after threats of violence' (Parry 2000: 33).

When jobs did not come through, people concluded that intermediaries had not passed on the money to the proper person, but had kept it for themselves. As Parry concluded, 'it [was] easy to see how the appearance of an all-pervasive corruption [was] sustained, even when the hands of those who [took] the decisions [were] clean' (Parry 2000: 33).

As already mentioned in chapter III.2.3.a, it is again insecurity which enables officials as well as middlemen to extort bribes from clients who are desperate for economic chances in an overall situation, as we must keep in mind, of high unemployment, even among the educated, low wages and an often dismal performance of public institutions which have to be substituted by costly private facilities.

While brokers are often portrayed in a very negative light, Corbridge et al. suggested that

> 'it [was] misleading to expect that development interventions [would] run smoothly in the absence of the pyraveekar [the local term for brokers] and his appetite for 'extracted benefits'. Inconsistencies [were] bound to open up between the 'vision' and the 'reality' of state interventions and this create[d] a space for actors other than bureaucrats to provide a service to local people' (Corbridge et al. 2005: 193).

Like Sudhir and Ranjit (compare chapter III.3.3.d), most of the fixers in the five villagers surveyed by Corbridge et al. were only 'small-time operators, [who] saw the state [only] episodically and through the narrow lense of the Block Office or the office/residence of an MLA'. A few of them could progress further up in the political hierarchy, but this demanded at least literacy as well as a lot of time and energy. Corbridge et al. summarised that those fixers that were looking for a 'career' in politics additionally needed

> 'to have a reasonable knowledge of the local political landscape and its rules, and a sense of how government work[ed] and [was] meant to work. Success in political society also depend[ed] on a person's ability to 'perform' his (or her) power appropriately, and to acquire a reputation for getting things done' (Corbridge et al. 2005: 196).

This takes us back to questions of accountability which will be discussed further in the following chapters.

III.3.3.f. Party Politics & Participation

The situation in the village studied in Debra Block, Midnapore District, in West Bengal was quite different from the one described above. Members of different parties resided in the village and actively assisted the poor in their encounters with the government as well as in conflicts with their employers. Corbridge et al. judged that party members had displaced the leadership roles formerly played by large landlords (Corbridge et al. 2005: 206). An account of a 'Gram Sansad' meeting in the village was presented in chapter III.3.2.d. While the leaders controlled the meeting to a certain degree, some villagers contested the figures for government spendings presented, pointed to failings of Panchayat members and proposed alternative plans. Especially, but not only, wealthier, educated villagers and members of the opposition party spoke out (Corbridge et al. 2005: 118). Even though most of the ordinary villagers stayed quiet, they might still be empowered by such meetings, as they can witness fellow labourers or neighbours speak up in opposition to the village leaders, argued Corbridge et al. (2005: 118-9). Their enquiries were handled in a civilised manner and the discussion was about rational and needs-based arguments. The leader's opinions were sometimes challenged and did not always prevail. These meetings, made mandatory by the state's Left Front Government in the early 1990s to increase the transparency of Panchayat decisions and enhance the accountability of its members, thus had the strong potential of strengthening citizen's self-esteem vis-à-vis the state (and other authorities) and 'reinforc[ing] the normality of the development state's active presence in village life' (Corbridge et al. 2005: 119).

However, as I tried to show in this paper, while institutions (or reformed laws or discourses on accountability) could provide new spaces of empowerment, whether these were seized by citizens depended to a large degree on local political as well as economic power configurations.

In another village in the same state, situated in Malda Block in Malda District, politics were clientelistic and state failure was widely remarked (Corbridge et al. 2005: 11). Corbridge et al. summarised:

> 'The same framework of political institutions [as in Debra Block] ... was associated with a very different pattern of social networks. A single Panchayat Samiti (Block-level) member cultivated direct and personal loyalty from people in the locality. ... Other figures were important by virtue of their control of Gram Panchayat programmes, but this power was also personalized in large degree. Although these new political representatives had displaced an earlier generation of high-caste village leaders, they had done so without producing public support for the functioning of Panchayati Raj institutions. Politics remained clientelistic, which is to say that services or goods were geared very directly to political supporters of the patron' (Corbridge et al. 2005: 107).

The CPI-M and opposition parties had a weak institutionalised presence in the village and political progression depended mostly on 'an individual's reputation for efficacy or even for violence, the two being linked in many cases'. By contrast, in Debra Block, political progression was bound up with the internalisation of values represented by the Communist party. As required by party culture, 'workers were at pains to demonstrate their hard work, commitment to the poor and 'simplicity'' (Corbridge et al. 2005: 196-7).

While in Debra Block, the ruling Left Front government as well as the local party organisation 'had done considerable work in preparing the ground for poorer people to participate in public meetings' (Corbridge et al. 2005: 142) and government programmes, citizens were not always eager to do so. What Corbridge et al. suggested in their evaluation of one particular government scheme (the Employment Assurance Scheme) can probably be generalised:

'sometimes [citizens] [chose] to avoid the project for good reason. It would take a considerable investment of time and effort for such people to learn the ways of the project and even then they could have little expectation of leading the groups they might join. In any case, the tangible benefits of project innovations seem[ed] small' (Corbridge et al. 2005: 142, 145).

Participation, they concluded had 'to promise something tangible if people are going to consider it a good use of their time' (Corbridge et al. 2005: 144).

In fact, trying to hold officials or politicians accountable in an institutional set-up that is 'out of one's reach', can even have detrimental effects. In Bidupur Block in Bihar, a group of farmers formed a committee to improve the situation in the local school. Since the primary concern was the teacher's repeated absence (compare chapter II.4.1), they agreed to visit the school on a regular base to put pressure on him. 'This effort at 'participation', however, had a perverse but not atypical consequence'. As villagers alleged, the teacher had bribed one of his superiors in order to be transferred out of the village. He also warned his colleagues about the villager's engagement.

'The result, according to villagers, was that several more teachers paid bribes ... in order not to be posted to the village, and the school was forced to close for several months' (Corbridge et al. 2005: 144).

III.3.3.9. Villager's Political Mobilisation

At Indepence, most of India's citizens could not access the political process, because of their disadvantaged positions 'in the overlapping caste hierarchy, agrarian system and local power structure' (Robinson 1988: 2). Democracy and new laws at first led to a reinforcement of the power of dominant landholding castes. They were normally the ones who were elected to positions of power (Robinson 1988: 2).

In 1988, however, Robinson judged that the situation in the countryside had changed and

'the rural elites [were] losing some of their powers, the agricultural overhaul [was] in process, and the vote banks [were] collapsing; these [were] related phenomena. ... The local elites [were] still powerful. However, ... they [had] been – periodically and significantly, if not systematically – assailed from both top and bottom. The resulting cracks [were] noticeable' (Robinson 1988: 10).

Robinson argued that one of the significant effects of changing power relations was the fact that poorer villagers got the opportunity to approach government officials directly (though with the help of a bribe) for their assistance in availing of government schemes – circumventing the village leaders. Before 1972, no bureaucrat would have helped a Mallannapalle villager without the consent of the influential village leaders. Robinson summarised:

> 'The Mallannapalle bonded labourers ha[d] not been released from servitude, but the system [was] changing and other options [were] becoming available. On the one hand, the old systems of moneylending [were] becoming riskier. On the other, government credit programmes ha[d] begun to reach the poor directly – by circumventing the elites, rather than by utilizing their 'good offices'. De facto, this often mean[t] that *the poor ha[d] increased their opportunities to bribe officials directly. This may not look much of a revolution from the outside, but the twenty-rupee bribe to a government official which [was] collected from twenty poor farmers rather than being paid by one landlord, signal[led] a profound change in rural credit relations (and in other aspects of the social structure).* ... In concurrent and closely related ways, the transactions between elites in their role as employers and the poor in their role as labourers [were] also changing. The poor ha[d] become less afraid. Thorner [1980 [1967]: 236] quote[d] the memorable remark of a permanent ('attached') farm labourer in Tanjore: 'Seeing the bejewelled wife of his landlord-employer walking proudly down the village street ... [he] called out: 'Madam, your ears are adorned with my blood'' (after Robinson 1988: 11, my italics).

Seventeen years later, in 2005, Corbridge and et al. concluded that

> 'political society ha[d] diversified and even democratized from its previously narrow base, and politics ha[d] effectively penetrated the villages of eastern India as a field of activity' (Corbridge et al. 2005: 198).

Although villager's participation in political decision-making varied widely in the five villages surveyed, in all of them 'politics [was] well established as a field of activity in and through which contests over status and other conflicts [could] be fought' (Corbridge et al. 2005: 116).

In Sahar Block in Bihar, where violent class tensions had only recently quietened down (compare chapter III.3.3.b, footnote 24) – after Naxalite forces had entered into political competition, and public hearings ('Janata Durbars') were institutionalised to defuse tensions – marginalised villagers, who knew officials from the Janata Durbars, had become more confident in their encounters with the developmental state (Corbridge et al. 2005: 116). During their visit, the research team witnessed a public meeting in which an executing agent for a Rs. 70,000 irrigation tank repair project was to be selected. A scheduled caste leader, NR, challenged the elite's candidate. He arranged for a number of women from his community to attend the meeting, therefore winning the election. Thus, the 'poorest and socially lowest group in the village [had] gained control of the tank repair project'. As this reinforces, 'a section of the poor is trying hard to get the state system working in its favour' (Corbridge et al. 2005: 117, compare chapter III.1.2.h). Such a direct challenge to the power of the elite was still quite dangerous, as NR knew. He could, however, rely on his community to protect him against retaliation by the uppers:

> 'The success of such tactics ... ultimately relie[d] on the understanding, won through years of agrarian conflict, that the Scheduled Castes [had to] protect themselves against the Bhumihars [local elite] when the state [was] not around to act as a referee. There [was] a saying in Bhojpur that 'only when every head is broken will everyone see sense', and the threat of broken heads [was] precisely what ha[d] force[d] some members of the Bhumihar community to concede ground to the Scheduled Castes when dealing with the developmental state' (Corbridge et al. 2005: 117).

As Corbridge and his research team summarised, the degree to which members of disadvantaged communities dared to enter into the political process depended on local patterns of leadership, past experiences and levels of political mobilisation:

> '[T]he degree to which the social networks of the poorest ha[d] been penetrated by [the state did] not simply reflect state-level differences in regime type, or the current institutional arrangements of local government. Important differences within Bihar and West Bengal [were] also shaped by the experiences of political mobilization, as well as of localized patterns of leadership and social dominance, and past government arrangements, among other factors' (Corbridge et al. 2005: 107-8).

Whereas recent literature on corruption often put special emphasis on the 'civil society', which is to hold politicians and officials accountable, there are no such civil society organisations in the villages surveyed, with the one exception of the Mazdoor Kisan Shakti Sangathan in Rajasthan (compare chapter III.1.1.c). Rather, as mentioned earlier,

> 'for poorer men and women, especially, and indeed for many government employees ..., the state [was] sighted in large part though the lens of political society' (Corbridge et al. 2005: 187)

and this is where questions of empowerment and accountability will have to be fought out, although civil society organisations – where they do exist and actively work for the uplift of disadvantaged groups (as opposed to simply 'eating' funds) – can be an important catalyst, as the case study of Rajasthan showed.

The last point to be made here is that politicians in all the settings had become accountable to their voters – though to differing extents and in different ways. Ideas of reciprocity were important to the evaluation of their performance as leaders. They could neither act as arbitrarily as the Reddy brothers had in Mallannapalle of the early seventies nor pocket *all* the money meant for development programmes without fearing the next election result. Villager's expectations clearly reflected this understanding, as Corbridge et al. analysed:

> '[P]olitical society ha[d] become domesticated in the minds of many villagers. The careers of political activists [were] linked from the outset to ideas of reciprocity, obligation and proper conduct which [were] constructed in part through vernacular idioms. This [brought] in to being understandings of politics that [were] most definitely not about ideology or policy preferences. Perhaps we can begin to understand the high degree of participation in local government affairs in these terms. Voting, or showing up to a public meeting, [was] in part a social obligation. It [was] an important public performance which, for all its hidden transcripts and 'backstage' denials, confirm[ed] the ongoing ties between lay villagers ... and party workers, and between both of them and the world of politics beyond the village' (Corbridge et al. 2005: 198-9).

III.3.3.h. Politicians Making Sense of Corruption

In all the villages looked at, political competition was intense, as political posts offered access to a significant amount of the state's resources in an overall situation of economic scarcity, low wages and high unemployment.

As the economic and political monopoly of large landlords declined, they tried to safeguard their power in legitimate as well as illegitimate ways. Important strategies were to run for a political post or to secure a job in the bureaucray. Political competition intensified, as leaders from other castes and social backgrounds also reached for political power, promising the voters to draw down development resources for them. The costs for contesting elections grew and many politicians used bribes accrued to finance them.

Rhetorically however, political players from all backgrounds condemned corruption and tried to use the general sentiment against corruption for establishing their own trustworthiness. Politically motivated accusations of corruption, transported by the media, made the topic highly visible and encouraged citizens to take action and hold leaders accountable.

For the subaltern, it was still important to stay in the good books of local leaders, but they also started to organise themselves in varying degrees. In some villages, the main success was that local patrons had at least become aware of the necessity to do something for their localities in order to be reelected, in other villages, even marginalised citizens became active in politics and party morals were high.

In all localities, however, politicians were certainly more accountable to citizens than previous village leaders had been, as the links between development and voting had become widely understood. What mattered to the voters was not how much politicians 'skimmed off' for themselves, but rather how much finally reached them and that they could access state services at all, even if they had to bribe officials and/or middle-men to do so.

IV. Summary & Conclusion

After Independence, the Indian state took on ambitious development projects, largely as a logical consequence of the arguments presented within the nationalist movement. Development became the *'raison d'être* of the modern state and the source of its legitimacy' (Harris and Corbridge 2000: xvii). Under Nehru, the first Indian Prime Minister, the Indian

> 'state was enlarged, its ambitions inflated, and it was transformed from a distant, alien object into one that aspired to infiltrate the everyday lives of Indians, proclaiming itself responsible for everything they could desire: jobs, ration cards, educational places, security, cultural recognition' (Khilnani 2004: 41).

The experience of rising levels of corruption, is on the one hand 'an almost inevitable corollary of the extended reach of the state' (Parry 2000: 52), and on the other,

> 'the postcolonial state has itself generated new discourses of accountability. Actions tolerated or considered legitimate under colonial rule may be classified as 'corrupt' by the rule-making apparatuses of the independent nation-state, because an electoral democracy is deemed accountable to 'the people' (Gupta 1995: 388).

In the Mughal empire, payments today considered 'corrupt' were customarily taken by officials as salary (Parry 2000: 52). Since the British colonial government was regarded as illegitimate, cheating it came to be admired as a 'patriotic virtue' (Bawa and Jain 2003: 16). Hence, the 'crisis of corruption' in India must be

> 'as much a product of a growing acceptance of universalistic bureaucratic norms as of its actual increase. Corruption has seemed to get worse

not (only) because it has, but also because it subverts a set of values to which people are increasingly committed' (Parry 200: 53).

It is therefore not paradoxical, but logical, that corruption is a threat to democracy and the rule of law, while it is precisely the

> 'rule of law and the legal-rational bureaucracy [which] gave rise to the concept of corruption in the first place' (Haller & Shore 2005: 7).

Especially in a country like India, where

> 'democracy was constructed against the grain, both of a society founded upon the inequality of the caste order, and of an imperial and authoritarian state' (Khilnani 2004: 9),

it is quite evident, that the promise of democracy – a community of equals, and the promise of development – well-being for all citizens, were made, *before* they started to be turned into reality.

While the benefits of economic growth, development programmes and public services are unevenly distributed, partly because elites try to safeguard their power and control over impoverished, dependent villagers, the idea of democracy is today at the heart of the Indian imagination, where it has

> 'begun to corrode the authority of the social order and of a paternalist state' (Khilnani, 2004: 17).

The 'deepening of democracy' (Corbridge & Harris 2000: 239) occurred because of several interrelated reasons. In Mallannapalle, local patrons controlled villagers almost completely until 1972 by virtue of their control over land and labour, the merchant's money and the Untouchable's physical force. Villagers feared them and voted as ordered in elections, so that village leaders could deliver vote banks to candidates at upper political levels. However, as the leaders' control over land and labour diminished because of new laws, improved implementation, increased competition for labour, improved communication and flow of information (through a new bus route and the media) and new sources for credit; the Untouchables and attached labourers ceased to supply force on demand. The village vote banks collapsed and villagers began to vote individually (Robinson 1988: 248). Government intervention, although limited and imperfect, was vital.

Even though officials that take the side of the poor against local patrons, might be transferred, their interventions set an example. The citizens witness that leader's power is limited and lose some of their fear – and

> 'what landlords most fear is a population without fear' (Robinson 1988: 259).

Political competition is intense, as the state has significant resources to distribute and there is generally high unemployment, even among the educated. As the state does not fund elections and new groups start to enter politics, the pressures to raise illicit funds to contest elections is great. There is also great demand for posts in the public services, since they are secure, when compared to the 'back-braking' jobs in the informal sector. The pay, however, especially for lower officials, is not very high and the areas to be covered by officials of the developmental state are vast. The pressure from fellow colleagues and politicians to extract bribes are high (they all expect their share), as well as pressures from citizens eager to obtain illicit benefits such as crop irrigation in out-of-zone areas. The procedural insecurity of citizens and government understaffing provide ample opportunities for middlemen to profit by assisting clients to obtain government benefits and keeping part of it for themselves.

While poor citizens suffer worst from corruption in public institutions (as in Palanpur), because they lack financial resources, the example of Mallannapalle showed that it was already a 'revolution' that citizens could access bureaucrats and development programmes independent of village uppers.

Officials and politicians are under pressure – both from superiors and voters – to spend at least a sizeable portion of development funds on what they are meant for. While they extract bribes mainly by exploiting client's procedural insecurity, some citizens, encouraged by the media as well as opposition politicians, take to defending themselves by appealing to superiors, gaining knowledge about rules and guidelines, or even lending support to social movements like the one in Rajasthan. Some enter into politics. It is political and social consensus on how much bribe-extraction is 'normal' and acceptable which sets the limits for rent-seeking behaviour of the elite.

As the discussion shows, corruption is certainly not a technical, but a political phenomenon, that stems from social and economic inequality, power struggles as well as economic scarcity and insecurity.

> 'The incentive to corrupt … is especially great in conditions of extreme inequality and considerable absolute poverty. Generally, corruption seems likely to be inseparable from great inequality' (Pavarala 1996: 110).

Caste or community affiliations are of little relevance when asking a middle-man for assistance, money is demanded from the majority with the only exception of very close kin. While caste is still important, it is 'more in terms of a person's ability to mobilize resources for a named group than in terms of abstract ideas about moral hierarchy' (Corbridge et al. 2005: 198). As Khilnani summarised:

'The conflicts in India today are the conflicts of modern politics; they concern the state, access to it, and to whom it ultimately belongs... Conflict is part of what democracy is: a raw, exciting, necessary and ultimately disappointing form of politics, that encourages people to make for themselves that most intimate of choices – to decide who they are and how they wish to be recognized, and to refuse to be ruled by those who deny them recognition. In India the idea of democracy has released prodigious energies of creation and destruction. Democracy ... as an idea, as a seductive and puzzling promise to bring history under the command of a community of equals – a promise that, given the inevitable gap between intentions and consequences, can at best only hope for partial fulfilment – has irreversibly entered the Indian political imagination. A return to the old order of castes, or of rule by empire, is inconceivable: the principle of authority in society has been transformed' (Khilnani 2004: 59-60).

While corruption is all about power, money and politics, recent discussions of the phenomenon have focused primarily on technical explanations and remedies under the umbrella of the 'Good Governance' agenda. I will shortly summarise the propagated instruments of administrative and legal reform and economic liberalisation for the Indian case.

Administrative reforms, such as simplifying procedures and informing citizens about their rights, can have positive effects and curb corruption, in so far as they curtail official's discretionary power, enhance accountability and strengthen the self-esteem of citizens. However, officials fail to act according to the rules not only because they hold procedural power, but also because the Block Offices of the developmental Indian state are severely understaffed and public servants are – in comparison with their counterparts in the private sector – underpaid. The reason is the lack of financial resources from which the state suffers.

Laws are an important point of reference in the media and in public discussions as well as in determining how far officials dare to bend the rules. However, India does not lack good laws, rather it lacks consistent implementation, again due to a lack of financial resources and the dominance of the elite, who alters rules and institutions to its benefit and often controls the civil services to a significant extent.

As Harris-White has concluded, 'the World Bank's project for the State', curbing the power of public institutions and 'freeing' the market, 'is the opposite of what is needed' (Harris-White 2004: 100-1), because public institutions, local infrastructures of rule and the implementation of laws need to be strengthened in order to be able to act as a check on the elite and to provide room for citizen's involvement. Presently, the numerous rules and laws for the protection of citizens and the environment are hardly implemented.

> 'The notion that further liberalization is the key to rapid and equitable development is wishful thinking' (Drèze, Lanjouw and Sharma 1998 (1): 226).

One of Parry's informants, 'an electrical contractor, with extensive experience of both public and private sector work', evaluated that corruption was the same in both areas

> 'But the difference', he went on, 'is that people do not mind it so much in the private sector. They do not think it is theirs' (Parry 2000: 53).

Privatisation and Liberalisation, far from promoting more efficiency and transparency, could instead decrease levels of accountability further, as it would certainly be the elite which would benefit; whereas other sections of the society lack capital to invest.

Politics is the main way in which more marginalised sections of society start to challenge structural inequalities which keep them poor and excluded:

> '[T]he poor are becoming ever more involved in India's politics and ... are pushing hard for a greater share of state resources ... the deepening of democracy in India offers India's 'social majorities' their best hope for taking some control over the economic and political structures which govern their lives and which might yet be made to work for their empowerment' (Corbridge & Harris 2000: 239).

In this respect, the poor are pushing the boundaries of elite's control, who reacts in numerous, often violent ways to protect its power. However, electoral competition and the media's advocacy help to set new standards of accountability, and

> 'contemporary concerns about 'corruption' in public life ... also help to define norms and standards for public servants, and - potentially, at least - provide for leverage for political activism. The state in India might indeed be increasingly rotten, but it is not accurate to say that men and women have lost faith, entirely, in the idea of the state' (Corbridge & Harris 2000: 202).

Neither new laws nor institutional reforms nor the 'discourse of accountability' created in the newspapers, politician's speeches, accusations, rumours and discussions among villagers, automatically become politically significant. Whether they do or not, depends on local circumstances and the 'level of organization of different groups that are affected by it' (Gupta 1995: 397).

Merilee Grindle (2004, after Corbridge et al. 2005: 184), writing about education reforms in Latin America, found that while most politicians were 'lukewarm' about reforming the educational system, and powerful forces were 'ranged in support of the status quo', change was still possible, but came

> 'in small and unexpected ways. Progress [was] rarely continuous, but when it [was] achieved it [was] because skilled reformers ha[d] been able to exploit general sentiments about efficiency and transparency to effect specific policy changes. These policy changes in turn [began] to change the terms under which succeeding debates … [were] discussed' (Corbridge et al. 2005: 184).

The same seems to be true in India. Powerful social movements, committed bureaucrats, politicians and journalists take steps to improve the system and the poor themselves, while still dependent on local grandees to a significant extent, they are encouraged to become active, to demand more accountability and to shape their own futures. While

> 'India is one of the few countries where the numbers of those below the poverty line have steadily declined, … there are still around 400 million Indians, mostly in the countryside, who are excluded from the channels of economic circulation and market exchange created since Independence. For them, little has changed. … So far, these hundreds of millions have been relatively inert politically; but as the idea of democracy seeps through Indian society, and as economic opportunities expand rapidly for some social groups in some locations, one thing that is guaranteed is the absence of a quiet idyll in Indian politics' (Khilnani 2004: 101).

V. Literature

Bawa, P.S. & Randhir B. Jain 2003, National Integrity Systems – Transparency International Country Study Report: India 2003. Transparency International. Berlin. Accessed on January 2nd, 2007.
http://www.transparency.org/content/download/1652/8377/file/india.pdf

Blume, Georg 2006, Die Zeit – International: Die neuen Kulturrevolutionäre. In: Die Zeit 21/2006. Hamburg, 11 pages. Accessed on January 2nd, 2007.
http://hermes.zeit.de/pdf/index.php?doc=/2006/21/china_xml

Brass, Paul 1997, National Power and Local Politics in India: A Twenty-year Perspective. In: Chatterjee, Partha (ed.) 1997: State and Politics in India, 303-335. Oxford University Press. Delhi. Series: Rajeev Bhargava & Partha Chatterjee (eds.): Themes in Politics.

– 1998, Theft of an Idol. Text and Context in the Representation of Collective Violence. Princeton University Press. Seagull Books. Calcutta.

Corbridge, Stuart & Glyn Williams & Manoj Srivastava & René Véron 2005, Seeing the State. Governance and Governmentality in India. Series: Breman, Jan et al (eds.): Contemporary South Asia 10. Cambridge University Press. Cambridge.

Corbridge, Stuart & John Harris 2000, Reinventing India. Liberalization, Hindu Nationalism and Popular Democracy. Polity Press. Cambridge.

Das, S.K. 2001, Public Office, Private Interest. Bureaucracy and Corruption in India. Oxford University Press. New Delhi.

Deccan Herald No year, Another Interview on the Gujarat Riot. In: Harsh Mander: an icon of courage and hope. Published by Drishtipat – Voice for Human Rights in Bangladesh. Accessed on 6th November 2006.
http://www.drishtipat.org/activists/harsh.html

Drèze, Jean & Amartya Sen 2006. India. Development and Participation. Oxford University Press. New Delhi. First published in 2002. Oxford India Paperbacks 2005. Second Impression 2006.

Drèze, Jean & Naresh Sharma 1998, Palanpur: Population, Society, Economy. In: Lanjouw, Peter & Nicholas Stern 1998: Economic Development in Palanpur Over Five Decades, 3-113. Clarendon Press. Oxford.

Drèze, Jean & Peter Lanjouw & Naresh Sharma 1998 (1), Economic Development in Palanpur 1957-93. In: Lanjouw, Peter & Nicholas Stern 1998: Economic Development in Palanpur Over Five Decades, 114-235. Clarendon Press. Oxford.

— 1998 (2), Credit. In: Lanjouw, Peter & Nicholas Stern 1998: Economic Development in Palanpur Over Five Decades, 506-583. Clarendon Press. Oxford.

Dye, Thomas R. & Harmon Zeigler 2003, The Irony of Democracy. An Uncommon Introduction to American Politics. Twelfth Edition. Wardsworth/Thomson Learning. Singapore.

Feiring, Brigitte (team leader; External Consultant to the Swedish donor organisation – Swedish Society for Nature Conservation - SSNC), **Shimreichon Luithui** (External Consultant to SSNC), **Anmol Jain** (Project Coordinator of the Indian NGO Rural Ligitation and Entitlement Kendra – RLEK), **Mohammad Kasim Khan** (Van Gujjar and RLEK employee), **Feroz Din** (Van Gujjar Representative, chosen by RLEK) 2002, Joint RLEK / SSNC Evaluation. An Evaluation of RLEK's work with the Van Gujjar. Unpublished, 25 pages.

Fels, Mira 2004, Talks and Discussions with Vandana Shiva and Wolfgang Sachs, during the one-week symposium 'Another World is under Construction: Towards Sustainable Forms of Prosperity' organised by Bija Vidyapeeth. Unpublished Field Notes.

— 2005, Development Projects in Northern India. Unpublished Research Report. (Based on Research in Dehradun, Uttaranchal with the 'Society for the Promotion of Himalayan Indigenous Activities', 21st to 31st August 2004, and Research in Amapurkashi, Uttar Pradesh with the 'Society for Agro-Industrial Education', 15th of August to 16th of September 2004), 80 pages.

Ferguson, James 1990, The anti-politics machine. 'Development', depoliticization, and bureaucratic power in Lesotho. Cambridge University Press. Cambridge.

Fischermann, Thomas 2006, Zerschlagen, nicht zerstört. In Houston endet der Prozess um die spektakuläre Pleite des Energieriesen Enron. Während die Exchefs ihr Urteil erwarten, lebt die Idee des Energiehandels weiter. In: Die Zeit Nr. 21. Hamburg.

Fuller, C. J. 1989, Misconceiving the grain heap: a critique of the concept of the Indian Jajmani system. In: Bloch, Maurice & Jonathan Parry (eds.) 1989: Money and the morality of exchange, 33-63. Cambridge University Press. Cambridge.

Glynn, Patrick & Stephen J. Kobrin & Moisés Naím 1997, The Globalization of Corruption. In: Kimberley Ann Elliot (ed) 1997: Corruption and the Global Economy. Institute for International Economics. Accessed on January 2nd, 2007. www.iie.com/publications/chapters_preview/12/1iie2334.pdf

Guha, Ramachandra 1989, The Unquiet Woods – Ecological Change and Peasant Resistance in the Himalaya. Oxford University Press. Delhi.

Gupta, Akhil 1995, Blurred boundaries: the discourse of corruption, the culture of politics and the imagined state. American Ethnologist 22 (2), 375-402. American Anthropological Association.

– 2005, Narratives of corruption. Anthropological and fictional accounts of the Indian state. Ethnography Volume 6 (1), 5-34. Sage Publications. New Delhi.

Haller, Dieter & Shore, Cris 2005, Introduction – Sharp Practice: Anthropology and the Study of Corruption. In: Haller, Dieter & Cris Shore (eds.) 2005: Corruption – Anthropological Perspectives, 1-26. Pluto Press. London. Series: Eriksen, Thomas Hylland & Jon P. Mitchell (eds.): Anthropology, Culture and Society.

Hansen, Thomas Blom 2001, Governance and myths of state in Mumbai. In: Bénéi, Véronique & C. J. Fuller (eds.) 2001: The Everyday State & Society in Modern India, 31-67. Hurst & Company. London.

Harris-White, Barbara 2004, India Working. Essays on Society and Economy. Series: Breman, Jan et al (eds.): Contemporary South Asia 8. Cambridge University Press. South Asian Edition published by Foundation Books Pvt. Ltd. New Delhi.

Hauschild, Thomas 2000, Bimbes statt Bimbos. Ob in Neuguinea, Italien oder in der CDU – überall entdecken Ethnologen die gleichen Rituale. Die Zeit 6/2000: 5 pages. Hamburg. Accessed on January 2nd, 2007. http://www.zeit.de/archiv/2000/6/200006.bimbo1_.xml

Hörig, Rainer 1995, Auf Gandhis Spuren. Soziale Bewegungen und ökologische Tradition in Indien. Verlag C. H. Beck. München.

Jayal, Niraja Gopal 2001 (1), Democracy and the State. In: Jayal, Niraja Gopal (ed.) 2001: Democracy in India, 97-100. Oxford University Press. New Delhi. Series: Bhargava, Rajeev & Partha Chatterjee (eds.): Themes in Politics.

– 2001 (2), Democracy and the State in India or What Happened to Welfare, Secularism and Development. In: Jayal, Niraja Gopal (ed.) 2001: Democracy in India, 193-224. Oxford University Press. New Delhi. Series: Bhargava, Rajeev & Partha Chatterjee (eds.): Themes in Politics.

Joshi, Abha & Mander, Harsh 1999, The Movement for Right to Information in India. People's Power for the Control of Corruption. Commonwealth Human Rights Initiative. Accessed on 6th of Nov. 2006.http://www.humanrightsinitiative.org/programs/ai/rti/india/articles/The%20Movement%20for%20RTI%20in%20India.pdf, 46 pages.

Kashyap, Subhash C. 2001, Preface. In: Kashyap, Subhash C. (ed.) 2001: Eradication of Corruption and Restoration of Values, VII. Sterling Publishers Pvt. Ltd. New Delhi.

van Kampen, Marcel H. A. 2000, Access to Development. A Study of Anti-poverty Policy and Popular Participation in two Squatter Settlements in Pune, India. Series: Nijmeegs Institut voor Comparatieve Cultuur- en Ontwikkelingsstudies (NICCOS): Nijmegen Studies in Development and and Cultural Change. Verlag für Entwicklungspolitik. Bremen.

Kansal, Utkarsh 2001, Why is corruption so common in India? Accessed on June 3rd, 2006. http://puggy.symonds.net/pipermail/corruption-issues/2003-January/000243.html, Link to: http://www.india-reform.org/articles/corruption.html

Khilnani, Sunil 2004, The Idea of India. Penguin Books. New Delhi. First published in 1997.

Krastev, Ivan 2003, When 'Should' Does Not Imply 'Can'. The Making of the Washington Consensus on Corruption. In: Lepenies, Wolf (ed.) 2003: Entangled Histories and Negotiated Universals. Centers and Peripheries in a Changing World, 105-126. Campus. Frankfurt am Main.

Kreutzmann, Hermann 1990, Oasenbewässerung in Karakorum: Autochthone Techniken und exogene Überprägung in der Hochgebirgslandwirtschaft Nordpakistans. Erdkunde 44 (1), 10-23.

Kumar, A. K. Shiva 1997, Poverty and Human Development in India: Getting Priorities Right. In: United Nations Development Programme India - Occasional Paper 30. Accessed on January 2nd, 2007. http://hdr.undp.org/docs/publications/ocational_papers/oc30.htm

Lanjouw, Peter & Stern, Nicholas (eds.) 1998, Economic Development in Palanpur Over Five Decades. Clarendon Press. Oxford.

Manor, James 1993, Power, Poverty and Poison. Disaster and Response in an Indian City. Sage Publications. New Delhi.

Matter, Dirk 2000, Indien: Wirtschaftsreformen seit 1991. net edition fes-library, 10 pages. Friedrich Ebert Stiftung. First published in Bonn in 1999. Accessed on January 2nd, 2007. http://www.fes.de/fulltext/stabsabteilung/00837.htm

Mendelsohn, Oliver & Marika Vicziany 1998, Subordination, poverty and the state in modern India. Series: Breman, Jan et al (eds.): Contemporary South Asia 4. Cambridge University Press. Cambridge.

Mistry, Rohinton 1995, A Fine Balance. faber and faber. London.

Mitra, Subrata K. 1992, Power, Protest and Participation. Local Elites and the Politics of Development in India. Routledge. London.

Murgai, Rinku & Lant Pritchett & Marina Wes 2006, India. Inclusive Growth and Service delivery: Building on India's Success. Development Policy Review. World Bank Document - Report No. 34590-IN. Accessed on January 2nd, 2007. http://siteresources.worldbank.org/SOUTHASIAEXT/Resources/DPR_FullReport.pdf.

Parry, Jonathan 2000, The 'Crisis of Corruption' and 'The Idea of India': A Worm's Eye View. In: Pardo, Italy (ed.): Morals of Legitimacy. Between Agency and System, 27-55. New York. Berghahn Books.

Pavarala, Vinod 1996, Interpreting Corruption. Elite Perspectives in India. Sage Publications. New Delhi.

Phukan, Sandeep No year, Profile. In: Harsh Mander: an icon of courage and hope. Published by Drishtipat – Voice for Human Rights in Bangladesh. Accessed on 6th November 2006.
http://www.drishtipat.org/activists/harsh.html

van Riel, Raphael 2006, Naxaliten. Accessed on 19th of December, 2006. http://www.sozialwiss.uni-hamburg.de/publish/Ipw/Akuf/kriege/232ak_indien_naxaliten.htm

Robinson, Marguerite S. 1988, Local Politics: The Law of the Fishes. Development through Political Change in Medak District, Andhra Pradesh (South India). Oxford University Press. Delhi.

Rose-Ackermann, Susan 1996, Democracy and 'grand' corruption. In: International Social Science Journal, Volume 149, 365-381. Blackwell Publishers. Oxford.

Sampson, Steve 2005, Integrity Warriors. Global Morality and the Anti-Corruption Movement in the Balkans. In: Haller, Dieter & Cris Shore (eds.) 2005: Corruption – Anthropological Perspectives, 103-130. Pluto Press. London. Series: Eriksen, Thomas Hylland & Jon P. Mitchell (eds.): Anthropology, Culture and Society.

Schmitt, Thomas 2006, Tausende indische Bauern gehen in den Tod. Spiegel Online. Accessed on 13th November, 2006.
http://www.spiegel.de/wirtschaft/0,1518,446922,00.html

Schneider, Jane & Schneider, Peter 2005, The Sack of two Cities: Organized Crime and Political Corruption in Youngstown and Palermo. In: Haller, Dieter & Cris Shore (eds.) 2005: Corruption – Anthropological Perspectives, 29-46. Pluto Press. London. Series: Eriksen, Thomas Hylland & Jon P. Mitchell (eds.): Anthropology, Culture and Society.

Singh, Karan 2001, All-Pervasive Corruption. Number One Problem. In: Kashyap, Subhash C. (ed.) 2001: Eradication of Corruption and Restoration of Values, 8-14. Sterling Publishers Pvt. Ltd. New Delhi.

Spiegel Online 2006, Geheime Kontenüberwachung. Bush beschwert sich über Swift-Veröffentlichung. Spiegel Online 27th June, 2006. Accessed on January 2nd, 2007.http://www.spiegel.de/wirtschaft/0,1518,423849,00.html

Stern, Nicholas 1998, Preface and Introduction. In: Lanjouw, Peter & Nicholas Stern 1998: Economic Development in Palanpur Over Five Decades, v-xvi. Clarendon Press. Oxford.

Theobald, Robin 1991, Corruption, Development and Underdevelopment. Duke University Press. Durham.

Tewari, D. D. 1995, The Chipko. The Dialectics of Economics and Environment. Dialectical Anthropology Vol. 20, Number 2. June 1995. Springer Netherlands.

Vittal, N. 2003, Corruption in India. The Roadblock to National Prosperity. Academic Foundation. New Delhi.

Wade, Robert 1982, The System of Administrative and Political Corruption. Canal Irrigation in South India. Journal of Development Studies 18 (3), 287-328.

Weber, Max 1976, Wirtschaft und Gesellschaft. Grundriss der Verstehenden Soziologie. Fifth Edition. First Book. J.C.B. Mohr (Paul Siebeck). Tübingen. First published in 1972.

Wolf, Eric 1977 Kinship, Friendship and Patron-Client Relations in Complex Societies. In: Guasti, L. & S.W. Schmidt & J. C. Scott & C. Landé (eds.) 1977: Friends, Followers and Factions – A Reader in Political Clientelism, 167-177. University of California Press. Berkely.

Ethnologie

Dagmar Siebelt
Die Winter Counts der Blackfoot
Mit Winter Count werden in der Nordamerikanistik die Stammeschroniken der Plains- und Prärieindianer bezeichnet, welche ursprünglich piktographisch auf Leder oder im Gedächtnis bewahrt wurden. Nach der Ansiedlung in Reservat(ion)en in der 2. Hälfte des 19. Jhs. wurden sie durch kurze Texte ersetzt oder ergänzt. Anhand der so tradierten Ereignisse konnte durch das Abzählen der Begebenheiten ermittelt werden, wie lange ein Vorfall zurücklag oder wie alt eine Person war. Diese Dissertation ist die erste umfangreichere Studie, welche die Winter Counts der Blackfoot untersucht.
Bd. 6, 2005, 472 S., 39,90 €, br., ISBN 3-8258-8240-3

Mongameli Mabona
Diviners and Prophets among the Xhosa (1593–1856)
A study in Xhosa cultural history
The South African anthropologist, Dr M. Mabona, uses the main title of this book as a convenient platform to launch an investigation into the roots of Xhosa culture and history. Many of the findings break new ground in Southern African anthropology and history such as: the original stock of the Bantu peoples arose from a cradle-land between the Orange and Vaal rivers in South Africa; the word 'Guinea' is identical with the Xhosa 'ebu Nguni' (Nguniland); Xhosa as well as Bantu history stretches back 50'000 years ago into the Middle Stone Ages (MSA) and into the Acheulian Age - the age of hominisation; the basic paradigmatic structure of Bantu speech; Xhosa thought structures; the fundamental relationship between the Xhosa language and mythology.
Bd. 12, 2005, 464 S., 35,90 €, br., ISBN 3-8258-6700-5

Andreas de Bruin
Jugendliche – ein fremder Stamm?
Jugendarbeitslosigkeit aus aktionsethnologischer Sicht. Zur kritischen Reflexion von Lehrkräften und Unterrichtskonzepten im deutschen Schul- und Ausbildungssystem
Ein ursprünglich für drei Tage geplanter Referenteneinsatz in einer beruflichen Fortbildungsinstitution entwickelte sich als Initialzündung für eine langjährige Zusammenarbeit mit über 1500 arbeitslosen Jugendlichen. Der Autor beschreibt den Weg zu einem Dialog auf „gleicher Augenhöhe" und zeigt auf, dass nur eine interdisziplinäre Vorgehensweise das Problem der Jugendarbeitslosigkeit lösen kann. Im Mittelpunkt des Buches steht die Fachdisziplin Aktionsethnologie und insbesondere die Auseinandersetzung mit Machtstrukturen, die einer konstruktiven Entfaltung junger Menschen im Wege stehen.
Bd. 18, 2004, 264 S., 24,90 €, br., ISBN 3-8258-7555-5

Peter Lutum (Ed.)
Japanizing
The Structure of Culture and Thinking in Japan
The aim of this anthology is to introduce the tradition of cultural blending in the modern and premodern japanese society which could be described as "Japanizing". This phenomena of cultural amalgamation of western and japanese elements is the basic pattern of japanese culture and thinking often with the result of an innovation in form as new products, new kind of ideas, behavior and styles. This concept of "Japanizing" could offer an intellectual approach for new interpretations of the japanese culture and society.
Bd. 20, 2006, 400 S., 29,90 €, br., ISBN 3-8258-8067-2

Peter Lutum
Das Denken von Minakata Kumagusu und Yanagita Kunio
Zwei Pioniere der japanischen Volkskunde im Spiegel der Zeitgeiststrukturen *wakon yosai* und *wayo setchu*
Diese Monographie untersucht das Denken der Volkskundler Minakata Kumagusu und Yanagita Kunio. Ihre Forschungen repräsentieren nicht nur die Anfänge der modernen Volkskunde in Japan, sondern in deren Intentionen spiegeln sich auch die mentalen Strukturen ihrer Zeit wider, die mit den Ausdrücken wakon-yôsai und wayô-setchû kategorisiert werden. Als zwei Konzepte, mit denen auch in der Gegenwart exogenes und endogenes Wissen hybridisiert wird, stellen die Begriffe wakon-yôsai und wayô-setchû Leitmotive in der modernen Kultur Japans dar und verweisen auf unterschiedliche Formen der kulturellen Kreativität.
Bd. 21, 2005, 360 S., 29,90 €, br., ISBN 3-8258-8068-0

Heidi Weinhäupl; Margit Wolfsberger
Trauminseln?
Tourismus und Alltag in „Urlaubsparadiesen"
Sonne, Palmen, Strand und fröhliche Menschen im Paradies: Inseln sind Orte für Träumereien. Und Träume sind der Rohstoff der Tourismusindustrie. Dieser Band blickt hinter die touristischen Kulissen so genannter „Trauminseln": Die AutorInnen beleuchten gesellschaftliche und politische Realitäten

LIT Verlag Berlin – Hamburg – London – Münster – Wien – Zürich
Fresnostr. 2 48159 Münster
Tel.: 0251 / 620 32 22 – Fax: 0251 / 922 60 99
e-Mail: vertrieb@lit-verlag.de – http://www.lit-verlag.de

von Zypern bis Rapanui und von der Dominikanischen Republik bis Mauritius. Kindersex-Tourismus ist dabei ebenso Thema wie die Traumata durch Bürgerkrieg und Tsunami auf Sri Lanka oder die sozialistische Utopie auf Kuba. Der Tourismus, als eine der Triebfedern der Globalisierung, ist häufig Teil der Probleme - und gleichzeitig eine der wenigen Hoffnungsbranchen für kleine Inseln.
Bd. 22, 2006, 296 S., 19,90 €, br., ISBN 3-8258-8638-7

Sylvia S. Kasprycki
Die Dinge des Glaubens
Menominees und Missionare im kulturellen Dialog, 1830 – 1880
Materielle Dinge befriedigen nicht nur menschliche Bedürfnisse, sie repräsentieren auch kulturell festgelegte Normen und Werte und werden damit zu Kennzeichen persönlicher und kollektiver Identität. Als solche spielen sie stets auch eine entscheidende Rolle in interkulturellen Begegnungen. Unter diesem Gesichtspunkt untersucht die vorliegende Studie die Konfrontation zwischen katholischen Missionaren und den Algonquin-sprachigen Menominees im westlichen Seengebiet Nordamerikas. Die Analyse der wechselseitigen Deutung, Umdeutung und Manipulation materieller Symbole in diesem kulturellen Dialog eröffnet Einsichten in die Dynamik des religiösen und kulturellen Wandels und erschließt die enge Verflechtung von Dingen und Ideen in der indigenen Aneignung des Christentums.
Bd. 23, 2006, 352 S., 29,90 €, br., ISBN 3-8258-8650-6

Gabriel Klaeger
Kirche und Königspalast im Konflikt
Christenviertel und Tradition in den Debatten zum *Ohum*-Festival in Kyebi (Ghana)
Ein Trommelverbot, das der Königspalast zur Feier des *Ohum*-Festivals ausruft, hat vehemente Debatten zwischen der *Presbyterian Church of Ghana* und dem Königspalast entfacht. Der Konflikt im südghanaischen Kyebi legt offen, wie beide Institutionen nicht allein auf dogmatische Kategorien zurück greifen, sondern vielmehr historisch-missionarische Errungenschaften und die Legitimität von „Tradition" einfordern. Es ist die Stellung des sogenannten Christenviertels und die enge Verflechtung von religiösen, politischen und rechtlichen Dimensionen, die den Kern der vorliegenden Ethnographie bildet.
Bd. 26, 2007, 152 S., 19,90 €, br., ISBN 978-3-8258-9725-3

Philipp Schröder
„Dagaalka sokeeye" – Gegen einen engen Vertrauten kämpfen
Der somalische Bürgerkrieg aus den Blickwinkeln ethnologischer und politikwissenschaftlicher Konflikttheorien
Der erste Teil der Arbeit diskutiert zentrale konflikttheoretische Ansätze der Politikwissenschaft und Ethnologie. Darauf aufbauend wird ein integratives Analyseraster entwickelt, mit Hilfe dessen „strukturierte Beschreibungen" von Konfliktphänomenen möglich werden sollen. Unter Anwendung dieses Analyserasters wird im zweiten, empirischen Teil der Arbeit eine Fallstudie zum Bürgerkrieg in Somalia präsentiert. Die Arbeit schließt mit dem Hinweis auf eine „irrationale" Dimension der Konfliktanalyse, verbunden mit der Aufforderung diese in zukünftigen Studien stärker zu berücksichtigen.
Bd. 28, 2007, 136 S., 19,90 €, br., ISBN 978-3-8258-9927-1

Alexander Kellner
Mit den Mythen denken
Die Mythen der Burji als Ausdrucksform ihres Habitus. With an English Summary
Das übergeordnete Ziel dieser Studie ist es, mittels Mythen der Burji zu einem tieferen Verständnis ihrer Kultur und Wertesysteme zu gelangen. Die Burji leben im Südwesten Äthiopiens wie in Nordkenia und sprechen eine ostkuschitische Sprache. Ihre Mythen enthalten keine dogmatischen Aussagen über ihr Weltverständnis, sondern bieten eher variabel auslegbare Denkmodelle. Es wird gezeigt, inwiefern eine Erzählung oder Erzählsituation bestimmte Gedankenanstöße evoziert und wie diese dann weitere Erkenntnisse oder Handlungsweisen strukturieren. Analysiert werden die in Originalsprache aufgenommenen Texte nach einem Verfahren, das hermeneutische und performative Ansätze sowie den Praxisansatz von Pierre Bourdieu miteinander verbindet.
Bd. 29, 2007, 448 S., 34,90 €, br., ISBN 978-3-8258-0051-2

René Tecklenburg
Die Verdichter – eine religionsethnologische Studie zum Schamanismus der Lakota
Die Verdichter ist ein breit angelegter Versuch, das religiöse Universum der Lakota-Indianer von South Dakota zu umreissen. Die konzeptuellen und philosophischen Grundlinien des religiösen Weltbildes dieser seit über hundert Jahren weitgehend erloschenen Kultur werden zusammengefasst und unter dem Aspekt geprüft, ob sich phänomenologisch dem zusprechen lassen, was die Religionstheorie gemeinhin als „Schamanismus" kennzeichnet.

LIT Verlag Berlin – Hamburg – London – Münster – Wien – Zürich
Fresnostr. 2 48159 Münster
Tel.: 0251 / 620 32 22 – Fax: 0251 / 922 60 99
e-Mail: vertrieb@lit-verlag.de – http://www.lit-verlag.de

Als religionsgeschichtlicher Beitrag verwebt *Die Verdichter* historiographische, soziologische, philosophische, linguistische und ethnographische Perspektiven zu einer Gesamtschau auf das Weltbild der stolzen „Nomaden der Prärie".
Bd. 30, 2007, 368 S., 34,90 €, br.,
ISBN-DE 978-3-8258-0362-9,
ISBN-CH 978-3-03735-155-0

Ethnologie: Forschung und Wissenschaft

Wim van Binsbergen; Peter L. Geschiere (Eds.)
Commodification: Things, Agency, and Identities
(*The Social Life of Things* revisited)
The empirically rich and analytically provocative contributions to this volume focus on Africa and on the process through which commodities come into being. Commodifcation is shown to be a powerful tool towards understanding the modern world, especially South economies and South-North interactions today. It greatly illuminates the three central concepts things, agency, and identities, and thus is conducive to the much-needed dialogue between anthropology and economics. In the book, some of the original contributors of A. Appadurai's edited collection from 1986 *The Social Life of Things: Commodities in Cultural Perspective* meet with today's prominent names in the field (Jean & John Comaroff, Paul & Jennifer Alexander, R. Dilley, M. Rowlands, and award-winning N. Rose Hunt) and with scholars of the next generation: B. Weiss, R. van Dijk, J. Roitman, J. Leach, and I. Stengs. Together with W. van Binsbergen and P. Geschiere, this team explores the dynamics of Commodification.
Bd. 8, 2005, 400 S., 34,90 €, br., ISBN 3-8258-8804-5

Eveline Dürr
Identitäten und Sinnbezüge in der Stadt
Hispanics im Südwesten der USA
Die Studie, die auf ethnographischer Feldforschung basiert, untersucht kollektive Identitäten, Repräsentationen und interethnische Beziehungen in zwei hispanischen Vierteln von Albuquerque, New Mexico (USA). Während im pittoresken Stadtteil Old Town Identitäten durch symbolische Praktiken öffentlich gemacht werden und zur Aneignung des Raumes dienen, sind im sozial schwachen Viertel Barelas kollektive Identitäten wesentlich weniger ausgeprägt und präsent. Die Studie geht den Gründen für diese Unterschiedlichkeit nach und stellt historische Entwicklungen, strukturelle Merkmale und räumliche Bedingtheiten in den Mittelpunkt der Analyse. Neben theoretischen Diskussionen liefert das Buch auch umfassende Daten zur Geschichte und Gegenwart von Albuquerque.
Bd. 9, 2006, 248 S., 19,90 €, br., ISBN 3-8258-9041-4

Julia Reuter; Corinne Neudorfer; Christoph Antweiler (Hg.)
Strand Bar Internet
Neue Orte der Globalisierung
Strände und Straßen in Afrika, indonesische Internetcafés und laotische Bergdörfer gelten bislang nicht als die zentralen Schauplätze der Globalisierung. Kritiker und Befürworter der Globalisierung schauen lieber auf das Treiben in internationalen Finanzmärkten oder in den Chefetagen multinationaler Konzerne. Materielle Infrastruktur oder gänzlich informalisierte, transnationale Räume werden hier weitgehend ausgeblendet. Der Band wirft einen Blick auf diese neuen Orte der Globalisierung, deren Bewohner ihren eigenen Umgang mit globalen Themen gefunden haben: Sie entwickeln Strategien, um die Lebensbedingungen vor Ort zu verbessern, ihre (Minderheiten-)Identitäten zu vernetzen oder weltweiten Protest zu organisieren. Neben empirischen Fallstudien gelingt es den Beiträgen aus Soziologie, Ethnologie und Politik die neuen Orte unter Zuhilfenahme postkolonialer, praxistheoretischer und weltsystemtheoretischer Argumente auch theoretisch zu ‚verorten'.
Bd. 10, 2006, 218 S., 19,90 €, br., ISBN 3-8258-9294-8

Franz von Benda-Beckmann; Keebet von Benda-Beckmann
Social Security Between Past and Future
Ambonese Networks of Care and Support
Social security is a particularly precarious issue where states hardly provide any services in periods of need and distress. The book analyses the arrangements relationships through which food, shelter and care are provided on the island of Ambon, famous spice island in Eastern Indonesia. It also shows how relations of support tie Ambonese migrants in the Netherlands to their home villages, and how normative conceptions of need and care among kinsmen and villagers change over time. Though special in their own historical setting, Ambonese networks of care and support are illustrative of poor rural populations in the Third World. Focusing on the precursors of the violent conflict that erupted in 1998, the book shows that social security is like a magnifying glass linking past, present and future.
Bd. 13, 2007, 344 S., 29,90 €, br.,
ISBN 978-3-8258-0718-4

LIT Verlag Berlin – Hamburg – London – Münster – Wien – Zürich
Fresnostr. 2 48159 Münster
Tel.: 0251 / 620 32 22 – Fax: 0251 / 922 60 99
e-Mail: vertrieb@lit-verlag.de – http://www.lit-verlag.de

Gerd Spittler
Founders of the Anthropology of Work
German Social Scientists of the 19th and Early 20th Centuries and the First Ethnographers
Work is vital for most individuals and for every society. Yet it leads a Cinderella-like existence within social anthropology. Even today we can learn from older social scientists like Karl Marx, Wilhelm Heinrich Riehl, Karl Bücher, Eduard Hahn, Wilhelm Ostwald, and Max Weber. Comparing industrial and non-industrial work, they were interested in the character of work as performance, play or ethical deed, and as rational action. Due to a lack of ethnographic studies, the empirical basis of their analysis remained weak. A serious ethnography of work was started by Karl Weule, Richard Thurnwald, and Bronislaw Malinowski. Having close links to the older social scientists they introduced new perspectives based on fieldwork in Africa and Melanesia.
Bd. 14, 2008, 320 S., 29,90 €, br.,
ISBN 978-3-8258-0780-1

Europäische Ethnologie

Cordula Ratajczak
Mühlroser Generationen
Deutsch-sorbische Überlebensstrategien in einem Lausitzer Tagebaugebiet
„Gott hat den Sorben die Lausitz geschenkt, und der Teufel hat die Kohle darin vergraben" – so umschreibt ein Volkslied die existenzielle Spannung, mit der auch die Menschen in Mühlrose umgehen müssen. Das Dorf in der Lausitzer Heide grenzt direkt an einen Tagebau, der im Laufe der Zeit die Lebenswirklichkeit der Mühlroser verändert. Vier Generationen stehen jeweils vor neuen Problemen und Chancen, jede einzelne entwickelt ihre Überlebensstrategie so wie ihr Selbstverständnis: „Rucksackbauern", „wendische Deutsche", „deutschsprachige Sorben" – was die Arrangements vereint, ist Ambivalenz.
Bd. 4, 2005, 256 S., 24,90 €, br., ISBN 3-8258-7000-6

Henrike Hampe (Hg.)
Migration und Museum
Neue Ansätze in der Museumspraxis.
16. Tagung der Arbeitsgruppe Sachkulturforschung und Museum in der Deutschen Gesellschaft für Volkskunde, Ulm 7. – 9. 10. 2004
Das Thema Migration entwickelt sich zu einer wichtigen Kategorie der Museumsarbeit. In Deutschland wird die Gründung eines zentralen „Migrationsmuseums" gefordert und gleichzeitig ein „Zentrum gegen Vertreibungen" heiß diskutiert. Auch andere europäische Länder entdecken den migratorischen Aspekt ihrer Vergangenheit und Gegenwart. Die USA, Inbegriff massenhafter Einwanderung, zeigen schon jetzt, wie sich Migration museal präsentieren lässt. Unumstritten ist: Alle hiesigen Museen müssen sich in Zukunft stärker mit der Tatsache auseinander setzen, dass Deutschland ein Ein- und Auswanderungsland ist und war. Dieses Thema anzugehen erfordert jedoch neue Ansätze sowohl in der Forschung (an Universitäten und Museen) als auch in der Vermittlung. Deshalb vereinigt dieser Band Erfahrungsberichte und Analysen von Volkskundlern, Historikern und Museumspädagogen aus Deutschland, Frankreich und den USA.
Bd. 5, 2005, 160 S., 14,90 €, br., ISBN 3-8258-8698-0

Martina Schommer
Binsfeld und die Base
Eine Gemeindestudie über den Alltag mit Amerikanern
Seit dem Ende des Zweiten Weltkriegs ist US-amerikanisches Militär in der Bundesrepublik Deutschland stationiert. Mehr als 15 Millionen Amerikaner – zumeist Militärangehörige – haben seither hier gelebt und das Leben in den deutschen Standortgemeinden in vielerlei Hinsicht beeinflusst. Am Beispiel des Eifel-Orts Binsfeld werden die vielfältigen Auswirkungen untersucht, die die unmittelbar angrenzende Air Base Spangdahlem auf den dörflichen Alltag hatte. Die Gemeindestudie beschreibt und analysiert den interkulturellen Kontakt von Amerikanern und Deutschen und berücksichtigt dabei insbesondere die Stereotypen und kulturellen Identitäten der Interviewpartner aus dem Ort.
Bd. 6, 2005, 384 S., 29,90 €, br., ISBN 3-8258-8759-6

Gabriele Ponisch
„ ... daß wenigstens dies keine Welt von Kalten ist ... "
Wallfahrtsboom und das neue Interesse an Spiritualität und Religiosität
Religion gilt aktuell als Megatrend. Die Institution Kirche jedoch verliert in Europa an Bedeutung. Elemente aus östlichen Religionen, Esoterik, Mythologie und Psychotherapie werden kombiniert und in die alltägliche Lebenspraxis integriert. Viele Menschen treten aus der Kirche aus. Gleichzeitig nehmen aber immer mehr an Wallfahrten teil, und auch die Zahl der Wallfahrten steigt kontinuierlich. Dies scheint widersprüchlich. Wie ist diese Entwicklung deutbar? Welche gesellschaftlichen Prozesse lösten sie aus und verstärken sie? Welche Sehnsüchte drücken sich im Interesse an Spiritualität aus? Auf welche Defizite verweisen sie? Welche

LIT Verlag Berlin – Hamburg – London – Münster – Wien – Zürich
Fresnostr. 2 48159 Münster
Tel.: 0251 / 620 32 22 – Fax: 0251 / 922 60 99
e-Mail: vertrieb@lit-verlag.de – http://www.lit-verlag.de

Funktion kommt Ritualen in diesem Zusammenhang zu?
Bd. 7, 2008, 296 S., 29,90 €, br., ISBN 978-3-8258-1070-2

Forum Europäische Ethnologie
hrsg. von Dorle Dracklé, Thomas Hauschild, Wolfgang Kaschuba, Orvar Löfgren, Bernd Jürgen Warneken und Gisela Welz

Michi Knecht
Zwischen Religion, Biologie und Politik
Eine kulturanthropologische Analyse der Lebensschutzbewegung
Als zeitgenössische Protestbewegung ist die Lebensschutzbewegung in der BRD in kollaborative wie antagonistische kulturelle Strömungen eingebettet. Die Untersuchung rekonstruiert die Anfänge der heutigen Bewegung aus der Perspektive ihrer Protagonistinnen und Protagonisten und analysiert, wie die Politisierung von Religion, die Sakralisierung von Biologie und eine moralische Rekonstruktion von Geschlechterverhältnissen zusammenwirken. Sie versteht diese Dimensionen als Elemente einer *Kosmologie in Aktion*, die auf die Transformation von Individuen und Gesellschaft im Feld emergenter biosozialer Phänomene gerichtet ist.
Bd. 4, 2006, 328 S., 24,90 €, br., ISBN 3-8258-7007-3

Alexa Färber
Weltausstellung als Wissensmodus
Ethnographie einer Repräsentationsarbeit
Wissen in der Spätmoderne ist problematisch geworden, folgt es deshalb neuen Produktionsmodi? Die Expo 2000 in Hannover ist in dieser ethnographischen Untersuchung der Schauplatz für die Thematisierung und Problematisierung von Wissen. Am Beispiel des marokkanischen Nationenpavillons und der Arbeit der Künstlergruppe BBM in der Themenparkausstellung „Wissen – Information – Kommunikation" wird dargestellt, wie im Kontext der Weltausstellung Wissen als Ressource, als Modell und im/als Transfer hergestellt wird und wirkt. Darüber hinaus geht das Buch der Frage nach, wie sich ethnographische Wissensproduktion in diesem institutionellen Umfeld positioniert. Dabei verknüpft diese Studie drei Felder der Repräsentationsarbeit miteinander: Politik, Kunst und Wissenschaft.
Bd. 5, 2006, 336 S., 24,90 €, br., ISBN 3-8258-8139-3

Elsbeth Kneuper
Mutterwerden in Deutschland
Eine ethnologische Studie
Eine Studie, die die besonderen Qualitäten ethnographischer Forschung demonstriert: „Mutterwerden" als Prozess, dessen „Natürlichkeit" angerufen wird, um kulturelle, soziale, technologische Eingriffe zu legitimieren. Ein Prozess, der durch Geltungsansprüche konkurrierender Wahrheitsregimes charakterisiert ist und an dem sich zentrale Elemente westlicher Kosmologien (Leitunterscheidungen, Leitwidersprüche) aufdecken lassen. Welches Wissen wird von wem wann wie mobilisiert, um eine spezifische Form der Körperlichkeit, der Subjektivität und sozialen Identität, die der Mutter nämlich, herzustellen?
Bd. 6, 2005, 320 S., 19,90 €, br., ISBN 3-8258-8114-8

Jana Binder
Globality
Eine Ethnographie über Backpacker
Durch intensive Befragung, Beobachtung und Begleitung von Rucksacktouristen aus der ganzen Welt war es Jana Binder möglich eine Ethnografie über in die Praxis Backpacking anzufertigen. Entlang des vielfältigen empirischen Materials wird gezeigt, wie sich junge Menschen durch diese Praxis distinktiv von anderen sozialen Akteuren ihrer Herkunftsgesellschaften absetzen: Sie produzieren Reiserepräsentationen, die beweisen sollen, dass sie sich in Globalisierungsprozesse einschreiben können. Dadurch erwirtschaften sie wichtiges kulturelles Kapital: globality. Zum ersten Mal wird Backpacking zu aktuellen Transformationsprozessen moderner Gesellschaften in Beziehung gesetzt und als Thematik begriffen, die entlang der Konzepte Transnationalisierung, Netzwerke und Medialitätzur Theorieentwicklung der internationalen Sozial- und Kulturanthropologie beiträgt.
Bd. 7, 2005, 248 S., 29,90 €, br., ISBN 3-8258-8686-7

Elisabeth Tauber
Du wirst keinen Ehemann nehmen
Fluchtheirat und die Bedeutung der Toten bei den Sinti Estraixaria
Inmitten der zuweilen vernichtenden nation-state-Dynamiken Mitteleuropas überlebten die Sinti als kleine, in ihrem kulturellen Erscheinungsbild unsichtbare Gruppen. Ihr Überleben gehört bis heute zu den ungeklärten Phänomenen der europäischen Geschichte. Die vorliegende Ethnographie zeichnet die zentralen Momente nach, die für die Fortführung einer von Außen selten erkennbaren kulturellen Kohäsion bedeutsam sind. Diese ist geprägt von den großen Themen des Lebens - Liebe und Tod -, die während und nach der Fluchtheirat der Sinti für einen kurzen Augenblick sichtbar werden.
Bd. 8, 2007, 296 S., 19,90 €, br., ISBN 3-8258-8816-9

LIT Verlag Berlin – Hamburg – London – Münster – Wien – Zürich
Fresnostr. 2 48159 Münster
Tel.: 0251 / 620 32 22 – Fax: 0251 / 922 60 99
e-Mail: vertrieb@lit-verlag.de – http://www.lit-verlag.de

Birgit Bock-Luna
The Past in Exile
Serbian Long-Distance Nationalism and Identity in the Wake of the Third Balkan War
In this study of identity politics, memory and long-distance nationalism among Serbian migrants in California, the author examines the complicated ways in which visions of the past are used to form Diaspora subjects and make claims to the homeland in the present. Drawing on extended fieldwork in the San Francisco Bay Area community, she shows how the Yugoslav wars generated a revaluation Serbian history and personal life stories, resulting in the strengthening of ethnic identity. Nevertheless, strategies for dealing with rupture and change also included contestation of exile nationalism.
Bd. 9, 2007, 264 S., 29,90 €, br., ISBN 978-3-8258-9752-9

Annemarie Gronover
Religiöse Reserven
Eine Ethnographie des Überlebens in Palermo
Der Mezzogiorno und vor allem Sizilien sehen sich von Stereotypen – Mafia, Klientelismus, questione meridionale – überzogen. Diesen stigmatisierenden Vorstellungen widersprechen nicht zuletzt die Antimafiabewegung und ihre Vorstellung einer Zivilgesellschaft. In dieser Bewegung spielt, was bisher kaum beachtet wurde, auch der Katholizismus eine zentrale Rolle. Die vorliegende Ethnographie des Lebens in einem Armutsviertel Palermos untersucht religiöse Praktiken, die sich aus den materiellen und ideellen Reserven der sizilianischen Gesellschaft speisen: Sie zielen auf eine Heilung und Heiligung der Menschen und eine Sakralisierung ihrer Umwelt, die sich einem von der Mafia durchdrungenen Sozialleben entgegenstellt.
Bd. 10, 2007, 240 S., 19,90 €, br., ISBN 978-3-8258-0395-7

LIT Verlag Berlin – Hamburg – London – Münster – Wien – Zürich
Fresnostr. 2 48159 Münster
Tel.: 0251 / 620 32 22 – Fax: 0251 / 922 60 99
e-Mail: vertrieb@lit-verlag.de – http://www.lit-verlag.de

Hans Jürgen Teuteberg / Günter Wiegelmann

Nahrungsgewohnheiten in der Industrialisierung des 19. Jahrhunderts

2. Auflage

Grundlagen der Europäischen Ethnologie Bd. 2

LIT

Grundlagen der Europäischen Ethnologie
hrsg. von Prof. Dr. Günter Wiegelmann (Münster)

Hans Jürgen Teuteberg; Günter Wiegelmann
Nahrungsgewohnheiten in der Industrialisierung des 19. Jahrhunderts
Bd. 2, 2. Aufl. 2005, 456 S., 40,90 €, br., ISBN 3-8258-2273-7

LIT Verlag Berlin – Hamburg – London – Münster – Wien – Zürich
Fresnostr. 2 48159 Münster
Tel.: 0251 / 620 32 22 – Fax: 0251 / 922 60 99
e-Mail: vertrieb@lit-verlag.de – http://www.lit-verlag.de